PUTNEY AND ROEHAMPTON PAST

First published 1994
by Historical Publications Ltd
32 Ellington Street, London N7 8PL
(Telephone 071-607 1628)

ISBN 0 948667 28 1
British Library Cataloguing-in-Publication Data.
A catalogue record for this book is available from the British Library.

Typeset in Palatino
by Historical Publications Ltd
Reproduction by G & J Graphics, London
Printed in Zaragoza, Spain by
Edelvives

PUTNEY AND ROEHAMPTON PAST

edited by
Dorian Gerhold

HISTORICAL PUBLICATIONS

Acknowledgements

Members of Wandsworth Historical Society who have contributed towards this book, by writing or otherwise, include Keith Bailey, Michael Bull, Nicholas Fuentes, Peter Gerhold, Pamela Greenwood, Janet Koss, Patrick Loobey, the late Don Pollock and the late Stan Warren. We would also like to acknowledge the assistance of the Putney Society in the early stages of the project, and the help received from the Wandsworth Local History Collection and the Wandsworth Museum.

The Illustrations

The illustrations listed below are reproduced with the kind permission of the following:

Bodleian Library, Oxford: *33*
Margaret Boxall: *100*
British Library (Althorp Papers): *63*
Michael Bull: *12, 16, 18, 21, 22, 39, 57, 61, 73, 75, 78, 95, 122, 127, 132, 136, 138, 140, 142, 144, 154, 160, 166, 168, 178, 179, 180, 182, 184*
Chorley & Handford Photographers Ltd: *191*
Terence Dalley: *9, 27*
Fondation Custodia (collection F. Lugt), Institut Néerlandais, Paris: *42*
Frick Art Museum, Pittsburgh: *74*
Nicholas Fuentes: *8, 15*
Dorian Gerhold: *17, 19, 30, 31, 90*
Peter Gerhold: *77*
Raymond Gill: *70, 71, 72*
Greater London Record Office: *183*
Douglas Harrod (Olney Collection): *2, 4, 26, 34, 36, 37, 38, 40, 41, 46, 47, 53, 60, 66, 80, 86, 98, 102, 114, 115, 117, 118, 139, 147, 148, 150, 171, 175, 176, 192*
David Haskell: *153*
Borough of Lambeth Archives Department: *24, 29, 173, 177*
Patrick Loobey: *7, 58, 91, 92, 97, 99, 101, 106, 109, 110, 113, 116, 120, 121, 125, 152, 159, 161, 162, 163, 165, 172*
Metropolitan Police Museum: *104*
National Monuments Record: *69*
National Motor Museum: *188*
Northamptonshire Record Office (Cokayne MS): *79, 84*
Michael Phelps: *137*
Private collections: *11, 28, 167 (by courtesy of the National Portrait Gallery)*
St Mary's Parochial Church Council, Putney: *35*
Smiths Industries: *187*
Wandsworth Historical Society: *14, 59, 169*
Wandsworth Local History Collection: *20, 25, 64, 65, 68, 81, 88, 89, 93, 103, 107, 108, 111, 112, 119, 123, 128, 129, 130, 135, 141, 143, 145, 151, 155, 156, 157, 158, 170, 181, 185, 189, 190*
Wandsworth Museum: *3, 13, 43, 45, 48, 51, 52, 55, 56, 67, 82, 83, 87, 96, 105, 124, 126, 133, 146, 149, 164, 186*
Keith Whitehouse: *50*
Wimbledon Museum: *131, 134*

Wandsworth Historical Society

Wandsworth Historical Society exists to promote historical research concerning the area within the Borough of Wandsworth. Its programme includes meetings, outings and archaeological excavations. It publishes the *Wandsworth Historian*, containing articles on historical and archaeological subjects, which is sent free to members. Information about the Society can be obtained from Wandsworth Museum.

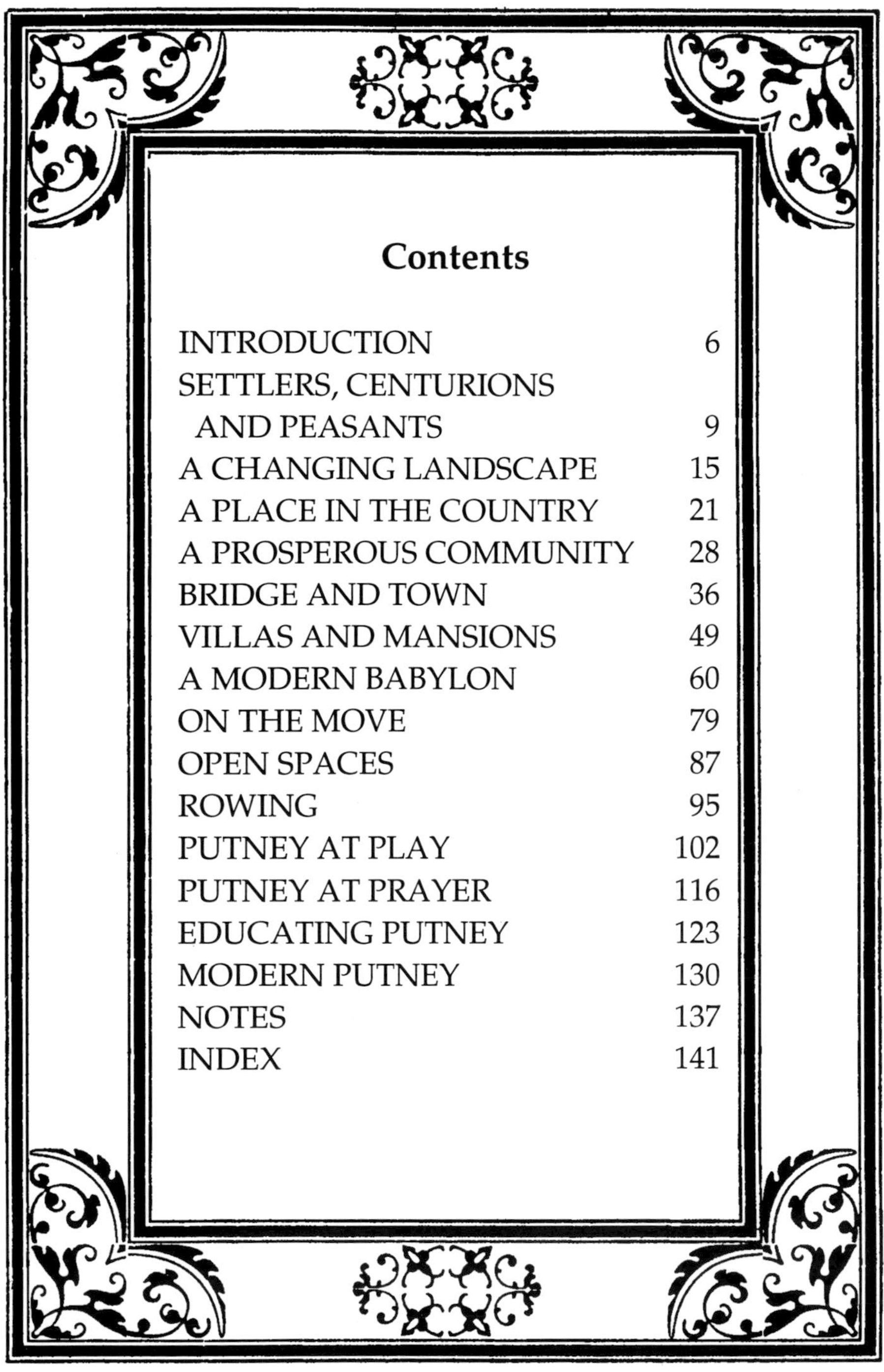

Contents

1. *Putney church and bridge, seen from the Fulham side of the river (engraving by W. Pickett, 1799).*

Introduction

The main theme of Putney's history has been the ever-increasing influence of London – the City of London being just six miles away. London was already making its presence felt by the time of Domesday Book (1086), when the manors in the north-east of Surrey, which included Putney, had the highest recorded population and highest number of plough-teams per square mile in the county.[1] There are examples of London's influence throughout this book, including gentlemen's and merchants' country residences, market gardening to feed the city, and eventually the building of suburban streets for commuters. Not for very many centuries has Putney been a self-contained town or village.

Another theme is the significance of Putney's position beside the Thames astride major routes to London. The Thames has played a substantial part in Putney's history: as a way of travelling to and from the city, as an obstacle which could be crossed by ford, ferry or bridge at Putney, as a means of making a living, and as a source of recreation. In the seventeenth century, when the importance of the Thames to Putney may have been at its peak, a third of Putney's householders were watermen.[2] The bridge built from Putney to Fulham in 1729 was the first permanent one across the Thames anywhere between London Bridge and Kingston, and its present-day successor carries more traffic than any other bridge in London.

The area covered here is the ancient parish of Putney. Strictly, Putney did not become a parish, as opposed to a chapelry within Wimbledon Parish, until about 1860,[3] but for centuries before this it was invariably referred to as a parish, even in legal documents. The parish stretched from the Thames almost as far south as the Wimbledon Common Windmill, near which there is still a stone marking where the boundaries of Putney, Wimbledon and Wandsworth parishes met. Beverley Brook provided most of the western boundary, and a small stream called Putney Gutter much of the eastern boundary – its course now marked by the dip in Lytton Grove, East Putney Station and the eastern arm of Deodar Road, where there is still an iron boundary post.

3. The tree-lined pavement in Putney High Street outside Fairfax House, where Montserrat Road now meets the High Street (watercolour by R.B. Schnebbelie, c.1810).

From at least the medieval period, Putney village was towards one corner of the parish, presumably because of the pull of the ferry landing, which, when first recorded in the seventeenth century, was at the bottom of the High Street.[4] One consequence of the way the boundary was drawn was that only a short stretch of river frontage was included,

2. Looking south along Putney High Street in about 1870, from between the present Felsham and Lacy Roads. The trees beyond the Spotted Horse on the right and the small buildings on the left (several of which still exist) mark the grounds of large houses.

4. *Putney from the river, 1878.*

offering far fewer sites for industry than in Wandsworth or Battersea.

The parish included Roehampton, often described as a 'hamlet' of Putney. There was a recognised boundary between Putney and Roehampton, and from the earliest records Roehampton had its own manorial and 'parochial' officials, though no church of its own.[5] Roehampton's history has been very different from Putney's. Whereas Putney's story has been one of steady and almost continuous growth, Roehampton has experienced sudden transformations every century or two, of which the building of the Alton Estates is only the most recent. Also, whereas Putney had excellent communications, Roehampton has always been more remote. It was a backwater until the seventeenth century, and then its very remoteness helped it to become one of the most exclusive settlements in the country, full of aristocratic residences.

Settlers, Centurions and Peasants

THE SITE

In general, the higher the land in Putney the less fertile it was. The highest part of the parish is the plateau which forms Putney Heath and Wimbledon Common. This is capped by gravels which give a thin, sterile soil, capable of supporting little more than heather, birch and grass. Clay forms the slopes below Putney Heath and much of Roehampton, and provided adequate pasture for animals but relatively poor arable land, being heavy to work and boggy. North of the clay, roughly from Howards Lane northwards, are gravel terraces which mark former levels of the Thames as it cut down through the London clay. These provided more fertile land, especially the gravel terrace known as Flood Plain, which covers the area between the Upper Richmond Road and the Thames. The Flood Plain terrace seems to have been the main area of prehistoric and Roman settlement, and was later used for market gardening. Its westernmost part, however, was poorly drained and became common land (Putney Lower Common) rather than farmland.

The most recent and most fertile deposits are alluvium, laid down in the last two thousand or so years by flooding rivers and found in Putney chiefly along the Beverley, where until the nineteenth century there were meadows and osier beds.

Water could be obtained from the Thames, from wells and from springs. The last occur where water which has descended through the porous gravels on the higher ground reaches the impermeable clay and emerges to the surface. For example, a spring near Putney Heath Lane gave rise to the stream called Putney Gutter. Two springs a little to the south of Roehampton Church School formed Roehampton's main source of drinking water until at least the eighteenth century,[1] though they have since disappeared.

Another important aspect of Putney's site is that it is the only place between the Strand and Richmond where the hillside with its gravel terraces touches the river's edge, providing a relatively firm approach for a river crossing, as well as a flood-free location for settlement. In the later prehistoric and Roman periods, and for long afterwards, the Thames at Putney was non-tidal, with its normal width (when not swollen by heavy rain) approximating to today's low tide, and there is likely to have been a ford at Putney in prehistoric times.

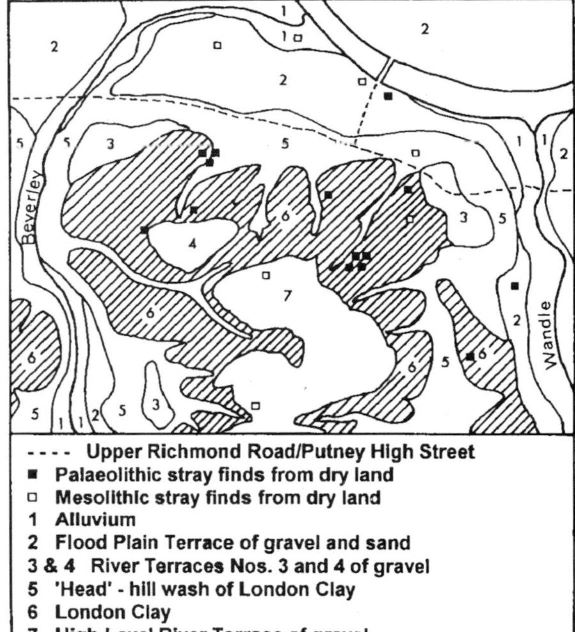

5. Geology of the Putney area, and location of palaeolithic and mesololithic finds (before 4500BC).

6. Contour map of Putney parish and the surrounding area, showing the parish boundary and neolithic and Iron Age finds.

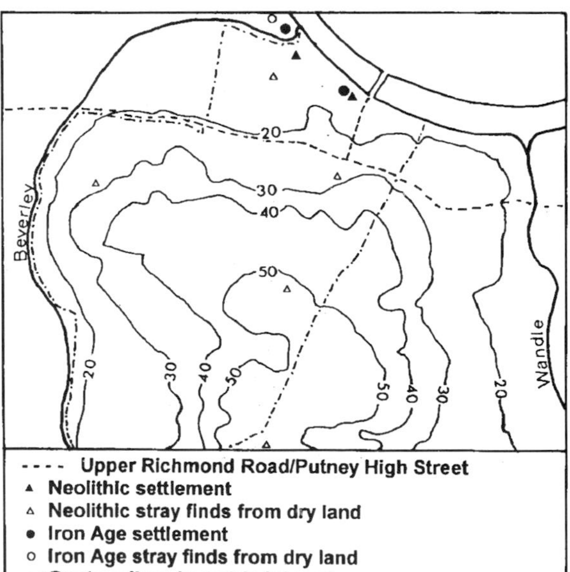

7. The conduit house (in the foreground) on the Common at Roehampton, built about 1630 and covering one of the two adjacent springs which provided the village's drinking water. Pipes from the conduit conveyed water to Sir Richard Weston's Great House (on the site of the Froebel Institute). In the background is Holy Trinity Church.

THE FIRST INHABITANTS

Finds during the past century and excavations carried out during the last few decades have proved that Putney has a history extending far back into the prehistoric period, although they cannot tell us how large the population was or whether occupation was continuous. The earliest direct evidence is flint hand-axes and flakes, some possibly as early as 400,000 BC. A small example from the Dover House Road area dates from about 28,000 BC. Between about 13,000 and 8000 BC, forests gradually developed as the Ice Age ended, and by about 7000 BC the London area was covered by dense forest, in which game animals were hunted using a new range of tools. Small flint flakes and blades of this period have been found in Putney, notably in Sefton Street and Felsham Road, and axes have been recovered from the Thames. Any settlement of this period would be difficult to detect, but there is an area of the foreshore near Putney Bridge rich in flint flakes of the type used between about 8000 and 6000 BC, where the Thames appears to be eroding a settlement on what was once dry land.

One of the most significant developments in human history occurred in Britain around 4500 BC, when people began farming and living a more settled life. For the first time there is excavated archaeological evidence from Putney, with finds from the whole of the Neolithic period (4500 to 2200 BC). People settled on the slightly higher ground, out of reach of the Thames, in a number of places from just west of the High Street to Sefton Street. A scatter of pottery and many flint implements from the whole period have been found at Sefton Street, and pottery, flint implements and a flint-knapper's hearth at Felsham Road. Fine axes found in the river may mark the beginning of the tradition of throwing offerings into the Thames.

Evidence is less plentiful for the Bronze Age (2200 to 700 BC), during which metal objects were made and used in Britain for the first time. From about 1500 BC the London region became an important metal-working and trading area, using the Thames as a major route, and this may have affected Putney. Most of the finds from Putney so far have been from the Thames, with no direct evidence of a settlement, but it is clear that people were in the area around Bemish Road, Gay Street and the Platt. There is a probable settlement site at Barn Elms near the mouth of Beverley Brook, possibly from around 1000 to 800 BC.

There is a variety of evidence from the Iron Age (700 BC-AD 50). A hill-fort a little south of Putney Parish – 'Caesar's Camp' or 'Bensbury' on Wimbledon Common, dates from about 700 BC. Pottery finds from Felsham Road in Putney suggest a settlement of the seventh to sixth centuries BC, although no signs of any structures have been found. As before, there are objects from the Thames: some particularly fine daggers and sheaths have come from the Barnes and Hammersmith reaches. A new development of the later Iron Age is the construction of large, often low-

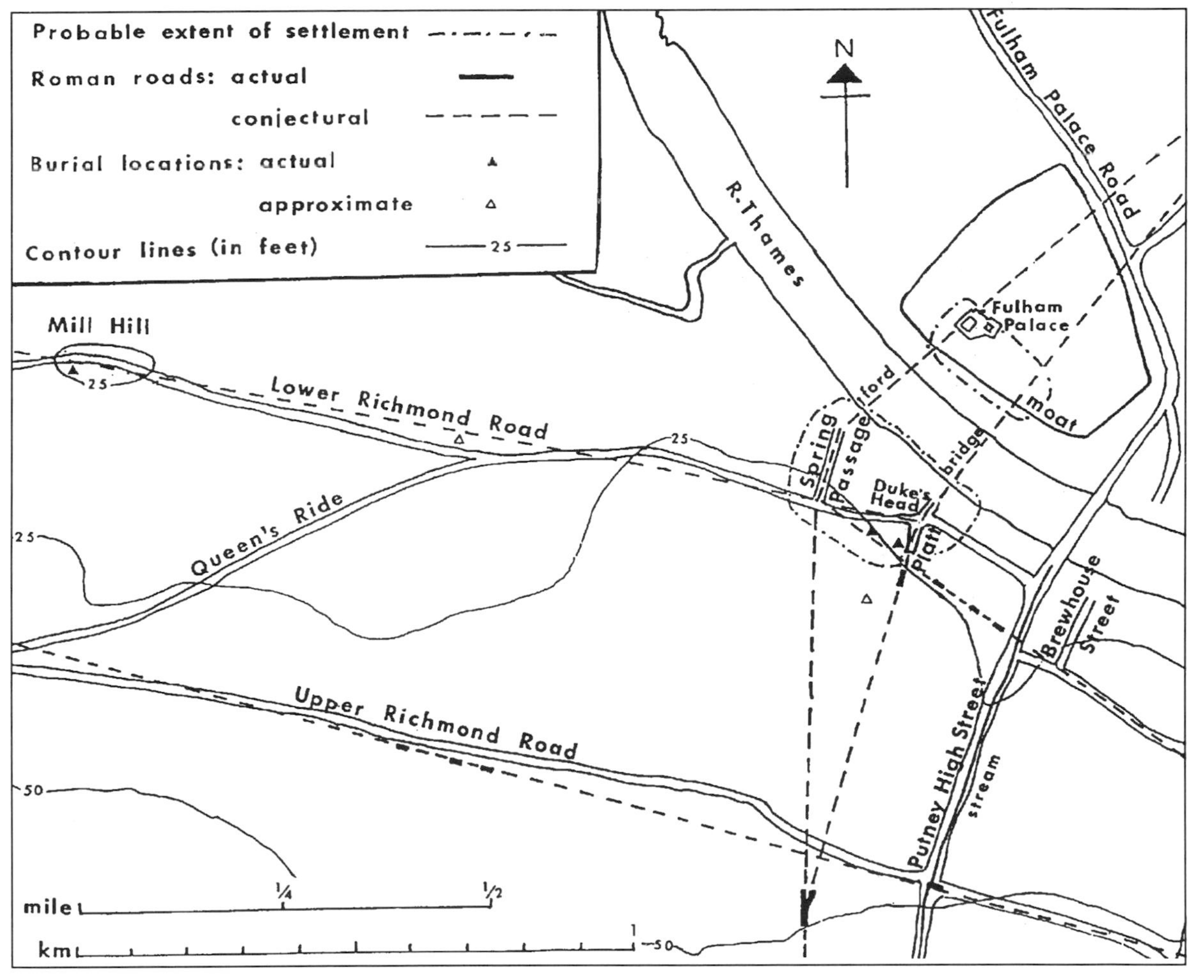

8. Conjectural map of roads in Roman Putney, by Nicholas Fuentes.

lying defended settlements, and one such may have existed at the mouth of Beverley Brook, where there was a meadow known as 'Rings Meare Hills' ('rings' being a name used elsewhere for hill-forts and 'hills' perhaps referring to ramparts). The former moat around Fulham Palace and associated earthworks may be a similar low-lying fort, as suggested by the size and shape of the earthworks and by the middle to late Iron Age pottery found there. (There was also Roman occupation there.)[2]

By the late Iron Age (about 50 BC to AD 50), settlement in the London area was probably as dense as in the early medieval period. A few pottery finds suggest a settlement in the Felsham Road and Star and Garter area, which continued into the Roman period.[3]

ROMAN PUTNEY

An important consequence of the arrival of Roman legions and Roman government in Britain in AD 43 was the foundation of London, which took place in about AD 50.[4] London's fortunes varied during the Roman period, but the city must have placed heavy demands on the surrounding area for food, stimulating the growth of settlements such as Putney. Considerable evidence of Roman occupation has been found at Putney, chiefly near the river in the areas of the Star and Garter and Spring Passage. The earliest coin found dates from AD 79, in Vespasian's reign, and there is coarse pottery which may date from the whole of the first century AD.

The complete plans of only two structures are known, both near the Star and Garter and both wooden and small. However, the occurrence of roof tiles, flue

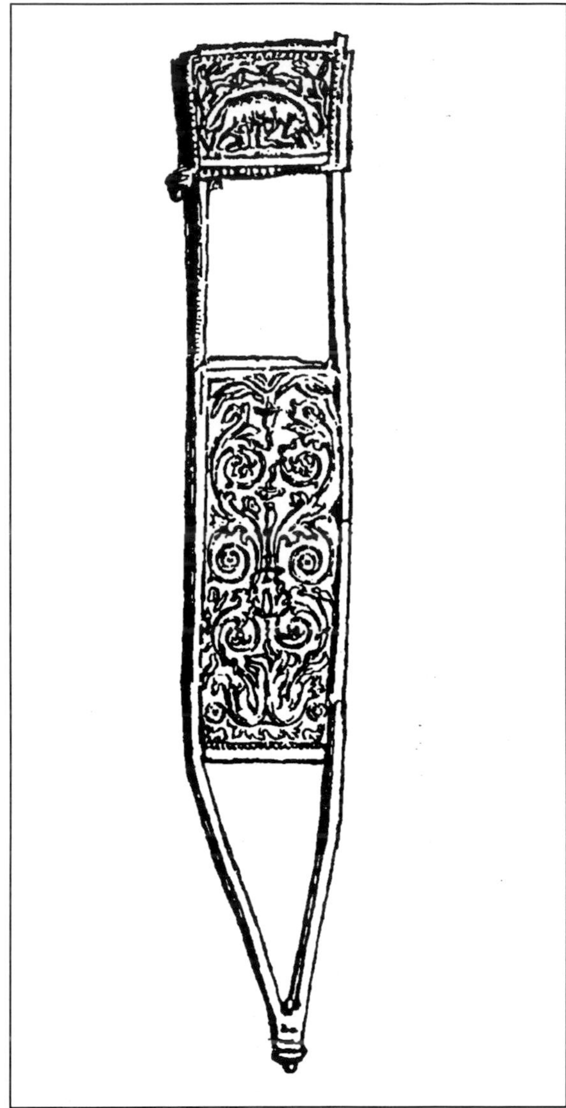

9. Bronze scabbard of a mid-first-century AD Roman sword found in the Thames between Putney and Fulham.

tiles and shaped flints indicates that there may have been some more substantial structures. The concentration of finds suggests that the heart of the Roman settlement was in the Star and Garter area, but it has also been argued that it could have been in the present High Street, near the later ferry landing, where there has been little excavation.[5]

A number of roads served the settlement, and a reconstruction map of these has been compiled, but many of the possible roads remain conjectural.[6] There is evidence for a Roman road along the Upper Richmond Road, roughly on its present course east of the junction with the High Street and variously 10 to 30 yards south of the present road further west. A ditched gravel road has been excavated in four places on this line, usually of single-lane width, and there is field name evidence from nearby Mortlake (a field adjacent to the road called Strat Furlong).[7] Evidence for the other roads consists of stretches of gravel, usually of single-lane width but in one case (under the Platt, which leads down to the river by the Star and Garter) about six yards wide. On the basis of the reconstruction, the crossing point of the Thames could have been opposite Spring Passage or the Platt (or both at different periods).

A case has been made for the area around London having been centuriated (divided by purpose-built boundary roads into 710 metre squares) for tax purposes, on the ground that London may have become a *colonia* in the late first century and that land around *colonia* was usually centuriated.[8]

The Thames was undoubtedly a major channel of communication, and this, together with the probable river crossing, will have affected Putney's economy. There was probably also fishing, and there was certainly farming. Animal bones indicate the presence of cattle, horses, pigs and goats or sheep, and a scatter of small worn sherds of pottery found over most of Putney north of the Upper Richmond Road and west of the High Street indicates that the inhabitants spread their refuse over arable land to maintain its fertility. The likelihood is that there was arable farming on the gravel lands and stock farming on the clay, with London probably providing the main market. Spindle whorls found indicate the spinning of wool.

Other objects found include bracelets and brooches; hair pins and bodkins; olive oil, fish-sauce and wine amphorae (large pottery jars from the Mediterranean area); flagons; quern stones (for grinding corn, from Germany and elsewhere); mixing bowls; cooking pots and Samian table ware (generally from Gaul); gaming pieces; military equipment; and a considerable quantity of iron slag.

A drawing of a pot discovered in one of the 23 barrows which once lined the present A3 west of Tibbets Corner, together with references to many Roman vessels being found in the same area, suggest that the barrows were Roman burial tumuli of the first or second centuries, but their location at the junction of West Hill and Putney Hill could mean that they were burials from Roman Wandsworth rather than Putney.

ANGLO-SAXONS

Coins and pottery indicate that the Roman settlement at Putney continued well into the fifth century. What happened after the Roman military withdrawal in AD 410 is obscure, although the London region appears to have been prosperous when Bishop Germanus visited it in AD 429. Very little evidence of Anglo-

Saxon occupation has been found at Putney, apart from a 'seax' (a type of knife), probably of the seventh, eighth or ninth centuries, unearthed at Felsham Road, and two others from the foreshore. There are no references in documents until 1086. However, this does not mean that Putney did not exist in the Anglo-Saxon period, since even more than in other periods it is a matter of chance whether evidence has survived. Moreover, historians no longer regard the Anglo-Saxon conquest as a cataclysmic event during which the existing inhabitants were slaughtered or fled, but instead as a more gradual process, in which estates and their populations were usually taken over as going concerns by a relatively small number of invaders.[9] London was again an important trading city by about 600.[10] We can therefore be reasonably certain that some sort of settlement continued at Putney, farming at least the gravel lands, and there was probably a small settlement at Roehampton too. The nearest Putney may have come to desertion is temporary flight at times of war, for example when Vikings spent the winter at Fulham in 879-80.

Putney is recorded in Domesday Book in 1086 as Putelei; in 1276 (the next reference) as Puttenheth; and thereafter usually as some variant of Puttenhythe until in the sixteenth century Putney becomes the usual form.[11] The standard explanation is that Putelei simply reflected the inability of the Normans to spell English place-names, and that Puttenhythe combined references to the Anglo-Saxon personal name Putta and the hythe or landing place, which would have been the settlement's most distinctive feature. Unfortunately this does not mean that a landing place must have existed since the Anglo-Saxons arrived, for place-names continued to change until the eleventh or twelfth centuries; indeed it has been suggested that Putney may once have been called Baston (the 'tun' or settlement of Bass or Bassa), the name of the field east of the High Street.[12] Nor does it entitle us to regard Putta, whoever he was, as the founder of Putney.

Another theory is that Putelei in 1086 was not an error but was the survival of the name of the Romano-British settlement, derived from the Latin word *puteal*, meaning the stone kerb or enclosure around a well or spring. This theory has itself been challenged on linguistic grounds.[13]

The name of Roehampton is even more unhelpful. It appears first in 1273-4 as Hamton, in 1318 and 1332 as Est Hampton (i.e. East Hampton, presumably to distinguish it from Hampton in Middlesex), and in 1350 as Rokehampton, gradually developing thereafter into Rowhampton or Roehampton. Rokehampton is usually said to refer to the nesting or gathering of rooks. Locally, the hamlet was known simply as Hamton, which has numerous possible meanings.[14]

More useful evidence is provided by Putney's field names. Several which appear to be of Anglo-Saxon origin suggest a pattern of dispersed settlement, possibly continuing the Roman pattern, rather than the single substantial village which appears on Nicholas Lane's map of 1636. They include Cadd Haw (Cada's Croft), covering both sides of the Lower Richmond Road west of the High Street; Tunstall (the site of a farm), next to the Lower Common; and Baston, east of the High Street.[15] There may have been other settlement areas whose names did not survive, especially at the bottom of the present High Street, which at some stage became the ferry landing.

Another piece of evidence is the existence of a detached part of the parish of Putney by the river in Barnes, west of Lonsdale Road, comprising 12½ acres of land. In the sixteenth century this was a meadow in which every holder of 15 acres in Putney or Roehampton was entitled to a portion called a 'lot', and probably it had long performed this function. Putney Detached is most unlikely to have come into existence *after* Barnes became a manor in separate ownership from Putney, which occurred in the reign of Athelstan (924-939),[16] and this suggests that the better resources of the manor were already fully exploited by the tenth century and equitably shared among the manor's settlements, including both Putney and Roehampton.

DOMESDAY BOOK

The Domesday Book of 1086 is a record of estates or manors rather than parishes or villages, and Putney and Roehampton are included in the entry relating to the Archbishop of Canterbury's manor of Mortlake. According to later evidence, this contained Putney,

10. The first documentary reference to Putney (as 'Putelei') in Domesday Book, 1086.

Roehampton, Mortlake, Wimbledon, East Sheen and Burstow (a detached part of the manor on the southern edge of Surrey near Crawley). The Domesday entry includes 80 villeins, 14 bordars or cottagers, 16 serfs or slaves, land for 35 ploughs, 33 ploughs actually in existence, a church and 'from the toll at Putelei xx s'. On the face of it the manor contained 110 individuals, which, assuming each represented a household of four or five people, indicates a population of about 500, distributed among six settlements of varying size. However, Domesday was interested in the resources of the manor, rather than population as such, and the 80 villeins, or tenant farmers, is probably a reference to 80 villein services (tasks such as ploughing the lord's land) rather than necessarily

11. The Richmond ferry, c.1770, the type of ferry which is likely to have operated across the Thames at Putney from medieval times until the building of the bridge in 1729 (drawing by James Marris).

to 80 individuals. If villein holdings had been subdivided, or villeins had employees, the manor's population could have been well over 500.[17]

It has been estimated that each plough or plough team in this period could work about 100 or 120 acres, depending to some extent on the soil. This would imply at least 3300 acres of cultivated land in the manor in 1086, compared with the 4600 acres of fields and enclosures (including some woodland) which existed in 1617. This suggests that very roughly three-quarters of what was cultivated land in 1617 was already cultivated in 1086, and rules out any idea that vast areas of land suitable for cultivation were unexploited in 1086.[18]

Putney was not wholly dependent on agriculture. The tolls at Putney were almost certainly income from a ferry across the river, and perhaps by this time there was river traffic between Putney and London. Certainly in later centuries the route by the long ferry from London to Putney and then by road into Surrey and towards Portsmouth and elsewhere (or alternatively by road to Fulham and across the short ferry to Putney) was an important one. For example, in the reign of Edward I (1272-1307), Robert the Ferryman of Putney and other watermen were paid 3/6d for carrying a great part of the royal family across the Thames, and also for taking the King and his family to Westminster, and the royal accounts suggest that the ferry boat was a substantial vessel capable of carrying large loads of goods as well as people.[19]

The Domesday entry for Mortlake includes a curious reference to a fishery which 'Harold established...by force before 1066 on Kingston land, and on St. Paul's land'. This seems to refer to a fixed structure of the sort sometimes used on the Thames, but it is not clear where it was. Whatever the nature of this 'fishery', it is likely that some fishing would have been carried on at Putney, since the river was later famous for smelts, eels and even salmon. With the resources both of land and river, Putney may have been a relatively substantial settlement in 1086.

12. *Haymaking in 1917 in the grounds of Exeter House (by Putney Heath), on part of the land known in the medieval period as Fern Hills.*

A Changing Landscape

OPEN FIELDS AND VILLAGES

The period from the eleventh century to the thirteenth saw three major developments which were largely responsible for the way Putney appears on Lane's map of 1636. First, it acquired a system of open fields, in which each manorial tenant held strips of land scattered throughout the fields and the cultivation of each 'shot' or group of strips was organised collectively. Roehampton acquired its own separate area of open fields.

Secondly, at some stage the pattern of scattered settlement in Putney disappeared, to be replaced by one in which dwellings were concentrated in the High Street. Since each landholder now had strips throughout the fields, it made sense to have the dwellings in a reasonably central location, though the importance of the ferry landing seems to have pulled the village away from the precise centre of the farmed area.[1]

There may have been a similar process in Roehampton, but later evidence indicates that the village was not where one might have expected it – on the site of the present village. Instead, it was in Roehampton Lane, roughly in the area of Downshire House, and the entire site of the present village was then part of the Common.[2] An earth bank marking the former boundary of the Common can still be seen on the north side of the Kings Head garden.

Thirdly, new fields were created on what had previously been common land or private woodland. This presumably reflected both the general increase in population, especially in the thirteenth century, and more particularly the growth of London, which provided a ready market for vegetables, fruit and other foodstuffs. In Putney, cultivation is likely to have spread southwards on to areas of clay such as Fern Hills (now part of the Ashburton Estate). Roehampton seems to have experienced much greater development. Fields which may date from around the thirteenth century include the Grubbing Ground (indicating grubbed up trees) east of Roehampton Lane and south of the Upper Richmond Road; the Breaches (indicating new cultivation) roughly between Bank Lane and the wall of Richmond Park; New Field, south of the present village; Stubble Field

13. *Part of John Corris's map of 1787 showing the medieval Putney Park (after the south-eastern corner had passed into separate ownership).*

14. The Baldfaced Stag (the tall building) and Newlands Farm (to its right), seen from the east in the late nineteenth century. Their site is now occupied by the Asda supermarket. The farm included all the enclosed land south of the present A3. It was a medieval enclosure, which had reverted to woodland by the sixteenth century but was cleared again in about 1630.

(indicating the stubs left by woodland clearance), south of New Field; and Newlands, in the Stag Lane area. Roehampton's cultivated area may well have doubled, and its population is likely to have risen to about 150, in about 28 houses, by the early fourteenth century, probably making it more populous relative to Putney than at any other time in its history.[3] Cultivation later ceased on some of the new fields, but none of them appear to have reverted to common land, and thirteenth-century expansion therefore did much to determine the present boundaries of the Commons.

Another new feature in the landscape was Putney Park, first mentioned in 1273-4. Its main function was to supply venison for the Archbishop of Canterbury's manor house at Mortlake. At least in its latter days it formed a rectangular area of 248 acres, with a lodge in the bend within the present Putney Park Lane. Its bounds were roughly the Upper Richmond Road in the north, the western boundary of the Dover House Estate in the west, Putney Heath in the south, and Larpent Avenue in the east.[4]

The date of Putney's first church is unknown. Domesday Book records a single church in the manor, which was probably at Wimbledon, but until the nineteenth century Putney Church was technically only a chapelry in Wimbledon Parish, and Domesday would not necessarily have recorded a mere chapel. Excavations at St Mary's Church (by the bridge) have uncovered a building which may have originated in the eleventh or twelfth centuries, and the church is known to have existed by 1291.[5] Parts of the original building may have survived until the rebuilding in 1836. There was no church at Roehampton, and its inhabitants attended Putney Church, which they reached by means of a path across Putney Park and the fields. Parts of the path still exist, for example as Quill Lane.

In 1332 there is for the first time a list of inhabitants, in the form of a tax list, although the 32 names are almost certainly an incomplete record.[6] Names of interest include William the Carter, William Hostiler, Stephen at the Well, and Richard of Puscrofte. Puscrofte, or Peascroft, was a field west of the bottom of Putney Hill, and indicates the growing of peas there. Two names provide evidence of medieval industries. John the Glazier was probably running a glass manufactory, though the size of his payment suggests it was small. In the fifteenth century there was a shot called Glazing Hall Shot west of the High Street, roughly between the present Lacy and Chelverton Roads, and the glasshouse was presum-

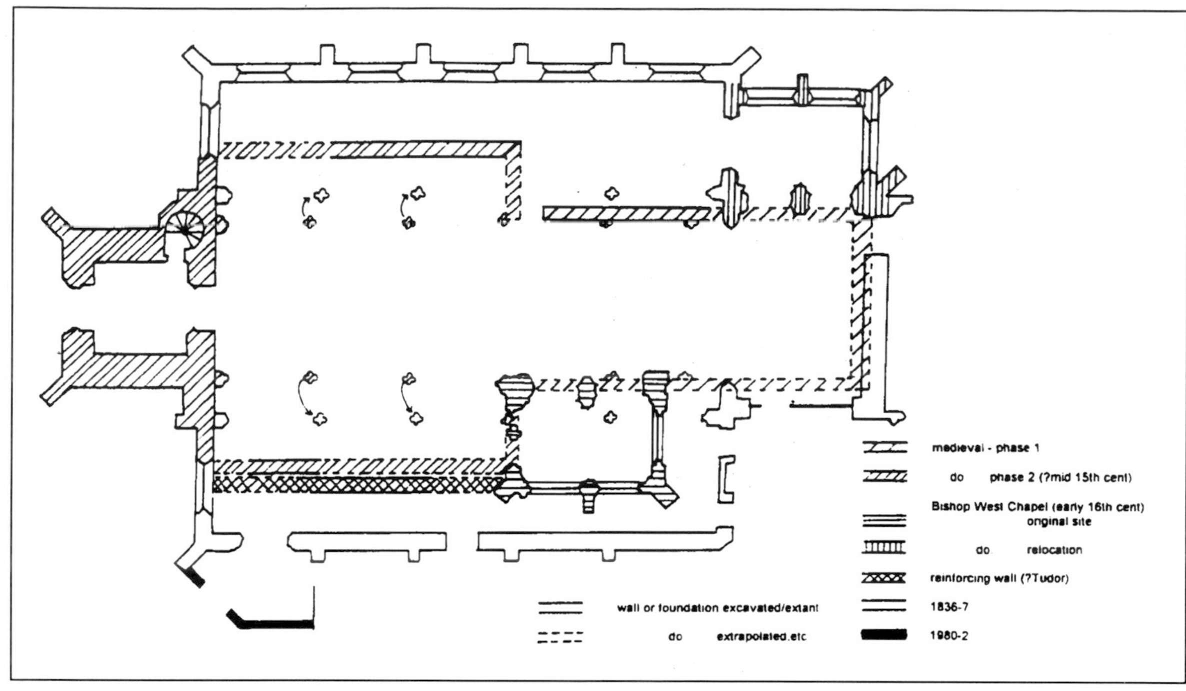

15. *Excavation plan of St Mary's Church, drawn by Nicholas Feuntes.*

16. *Demolition of St Mary's Church, 4 March 1836, showing the medieval columns and Bishop West's Chapel, which were incorporated in the present building on different sites. (Lithograph based on drawing by E. Bradley.)*

17. *Quill Lane, part of the medieval church path from Roehampton.*

18. *The fifteenth-century tower of St Mary's Church, seen from the Lower Richmond Road (watercolour, c.1810).*

ably there. Martin the Brewer was the third largest taxpayer, which suggests that he ran the substantial brewery which existed until about 1700 by the river east of Brewhouse Lane; in the seventeenth century it was supplying customers as far away as Battersea and Lambeth.

Following the arrival of the Black Death in 1348, the newer and less fertile fields such as Fern Hills were abandoned, becoming known as the 'wild lands', and the local population fell drastically, especially in Roehampton. A manorial survey of 1497, by which time there had probably been some recovery, records 28 hempstalls or dwelling sites in Roehampton, but 14 of these were 'an hempstall withoute an house'.[7]

The building of the tower of St Mary's, dated on architectural grounds to about 1450, can be taken as a sign of returning prosperity. At about that time the 'wild lands' began to be reclaimed and enclosures began to be made. In 1474, for example, Fern Hills, which was lying waste and overgrown, was enclosed and divided by agreement of the tenants. Other enclosures caused disputes, and several riots are recorded.[8] The most vigorous encloser was John Twigge, a member of the Grocers' Company of the City of London; he was also connected with the Merchants of the Staple at Calais, who were large-scale wool traders, and most of his enclosures were probably for sheep grazing. The largest was the Pightells, the area bounded roughly by Dyers Lane, the Lower Common, Dryburgh and Erpingham Roads, and the Upper Richmond Road. At least part of this area was enclosed by Twigge in 1469, and it was probably taken from the Lower Common, halving its area.

PUTNEY IN 1497

Detailed surveys of Putney and Roehampton survive from 1497, listing every house and every strip in the fields and making it possible to reconstruct most of the landscape as it existed at the end of the Middle Ages.[9] 48 dwellings are recorded in Putney, indicating a population of about 300. The buildings are harder to identify than the fields, but it is likely that nearly all were in the High Street or on the riverside nearest it. Several are of particular interest, especially the five 'chief places' or mansions discussed in the next chapter. There were also 'the beerhouse', belonging to Richard Welbeck, and the 'Katheryn Whele', which was presumably an inn. All these provided non-agricultural employment, as did the river. The ferry continued to be well patronised by royalty, and the people of Putney were clearly familiar with the sight of the country's rulers passing through their village. For example, Henry VIII incurred expenses of 10s. 8d. in June 1531 for 'the King's watermen waiting with the barge to Putney with 16 men', and in

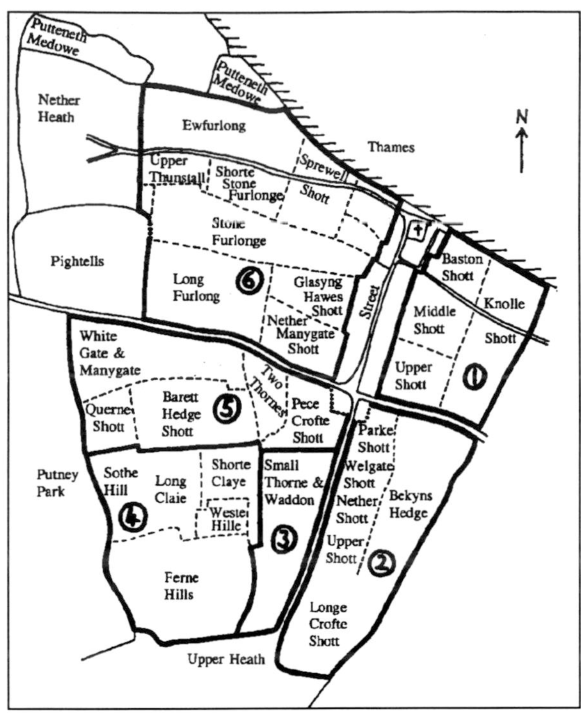

19. Putney's open fields in 1497. Heavy lines indicate the six fields; broken lines indicate the shots or furlongs.

August 1544 the Queen (Katherine Parr) paid 8d. boat hire from Westminster to Putney when removing to Hampton Court. A few years earlier, in 1529, Henry VIII's disgraced chief minister, Cardinal Wolsey, came by barge from Westminster to Putney when ordered to retire to his seat at Esher. In Putney High Street he was met by Henry Norris bearing a cheering message from the King and a gold ring as a token, whereupon Wolsey leapt from his mule and 'kneeled down in the dirt upon both his knees, holding up his hands for joy'.[10]

Instead of the 'three field' system of the history textbooks, Putney had six fields of differing sizes in 1497: Baston (70½ acres), Coalecroft (94¼), Smallthorn and Waddon(42¾), Fourth (86½), Fifth (88¼), and Sixth (217¼), making a total of 599½ acres (including 119 acres of private closes). Furthermore, the unit of cultivation in Putney (as elsewhere), within which all landholders had to grow the same crop or leave fallow, was not the field but the furlong or shott, ranging in size from 5 to 40 acres. After the harvest, animals were kept on the open fields, where they helped to fertilize the soil, but during the rest of the year they grazed either in private closes or on the Commons. The farmers also required meadow land, to provide the hay which sustained their livestock during the winter. Some landholders held parts of Putney Meadow, which lay along the south side of Beverley Brook, but there was also Lottmead, in Barnes, which continued to be divided up and allocated among the landholders of Putney and Roehampton every year until about 1640. Dung was brought from London in large quantities to increase the fertility of the fields, and by 1604 there was a dung wharf carefully placed in the extreme north-east corner of the parish so that the prevailing winds would blow offensive smells into neighbouring parishes.[11] The system of open fields and commons was regulated by the manor court, which comprised manorial tenants from all parts of the manor.

Roehampton's 14 houses in 1497 suggest a population of about 80, only a quarter of that in Putney. Roehampton had about 280 acres of open fields, stretching (in modern terms) approximately from Priory Lane in the west to the western boundary of the Dover House Estate in the east, and from the Bank of England sports pavilion in the north to the Richmond Park wall in the south. There were also private closes and woods.[12]

The medieval landscape disappeared sooner in Roehampton than in Putney. In about 1568 its open fields were enclosed 'by mutual consent and agreement'.[13] The village subsequently expanded northwards along Roehampton Lane, and by 1617 there were 30 houses. In or shortly before 1597, Thomas Jennings unlawfully erected a cottage on the Common near the Buck Pound, which seems to have been near the Kings Head.[14] This was one of the first of the cottages which in the seventeenth century were to multiply and become a new village, occupying the site of present-day Roehampton village.

Putney also grew rapidly in the sixteenth century, from 48 houses in 1497 to just over a hundred in 1617, but this growth was accommodated almost entirely within the existing built-up area, and the open fields remained largely unenclosed until the 1630s and 1640s.

A Place in the Country

The five 'chief places' or mansions listed in 1497 made Putney an unusual settlement. Other areas regarded as Londoners' playgrounds, such as Hampstead, did not develop significantly until the seventeenth century.[1] The names of some of the mansions' occupiers can be obtained from monumental inscriptions and wills. Some were government officials: men like John Wykys, Usher of the Chamber to Henry VII (and father-in-law of Thomas Cromwell); William Whorwood, Attorney General to Henry VIII; and Sir Richard Brooke, Lord Chief Baron of the Exchequer under Henry VIII, who kept horses for riding in Putney Park. Probably outnumbering these were London merchants, such as Richard Twigge, mercer and merchant of the Calais Staple. Before the Reformation there were sometimes servants of the Archbishop of Canterbury, who had a manor house at Mortlake; they included John Urtwayte, Clerk of the Kitchen to Cardinal Morton in the late fifteeenth century. Another exotic local resident was Anthony Woodville, Earl Rivers, brother-in-law of Edward IV, who translated from French the first book to be printed in England in English; he was executed in 1483 by Richard III.

Some of the chief places of 1497 can be identified. By the river, on the westernmost part of the present Kenilworth Court site, was that of William Welbeck, a member of the Haberdashers' Company and a sheriff of London in 1492. The Welbecks are recorded in Putney from the early 1460s to 1558, and also had land at West Peckham in Kent. The chief place of Thomas Rich stood on the easternmost part of the Kenilworth Court site, and part of it may have survived until the nineteenth century.

The most important of the chief places seems to have been Upper Place (later known as Coalecroft or Lime Grove), which stood at the bottom of Putney Hill on the east side and belonged in 1497 to Richard Twigge. John Twigge had earlier made great efforts to improve its grounds, including the diversion into a series of ponds of the stream which fed Putney's 'common gutter' through the High Street. As a result, 'scarcely any water in summer time comes from that spring into the common gutter of the town, to the prejudice and to the great danger of the town, which might happen for want of water.' (Nevertheless, the High Street stream is recorded in subsequent centuries and even now a trickle of water continues to emerge under Putney Bridge). In 1497 the Twigges held about 55% of all Putney's farmland, together with nearly a third of the dwellings and some land in Roehampton; they also had land in Kent. However, the Twigges, first recorded in Putney in 1459, do not appear at all in local records after 1511. A feature of

20. A house built in about 1530 around a courtyard east of Putney High Street opposite Felsham Road (watercolour, c.1810).

21. Brass of John and Agnes Welbeck, who lived in a mansion on the site of the present Kenilworth Court and died in 1476 and 1478 (engraving). Only the inscription and the stone matrix survive.

22. Bishop West's chantry chapel, before rebuilding (lithograph, 1823).

sixteenth and seventeenth-century Putney was rapid changes of ownership as estates were built up and then transferred or dispersed; there were no great Putney dynasties spanning many generations. The next recorded occupant of Upper Place was Ralph Dodmer, Lord Mayor of London in 1529. By the end of the century the estate included a series of enclosed fields extending to the top of the Hill.

NICHOLAS WEST AND THOMAS CROMWELL

Other families in the late fifteenth century produced two of Putney's most famous sons – Nicholas West and Thomas Cromwell. West was born in the 1460s, the son of a baker, Thomas West, who in 1497 held 26 acres and four houses in Putney. Nicholas became a student at King's College, Cambridge, where, among other pranks, he set fire to the Provost's lodging, for which he was expelled. However, he made good, becoming an eminent scholar and statesman, and Henry VIII made him Bishop of Ely. He died in 1533, having already built two splendid chantry chapels at Ely Cathedral and Putney, in which masses were to be said for the repose of his soul.[2] Both survive, though the Putney chapel was reconstructed in a different part of the church in the nineteenth century.

The Cromwell family came from Nottinghamshire, and is first recorded locally in the 1450s. Walter Cromwell, father of Thomas, is variously described as smith, brewer and fuller, and perhaps carried out all three trades at different times or together, becoming intermittently prosperous. He was a disorderly character, constantly in trouble with the manor court for over-burdening the Commons with his livestock, for cutting too much furze and thorns, and even for assault. In 1514 he forfeited all his lands for tampering with the manorial records.[3]

His son Thomas was probably only a boy when he left Putney, and is said to have admitted later 'what a ruffian he was in his younger days'.[4] In the 1520s he was in the service of Cardinal Wolsey, and his rise after Wolsey's fall was meteoric, making him Henry VIII's chief minister for a decade: 'perhaps the most accomplished servant any English monarch has enjoyed, a royal minister who cut a deeper mark on the history of England than have many of her monarchs', according to one historian.[5] Among the measures he carried through were the dissolution of the monasteries, the publication of an English Bible, and in 1538 the introduction of parish registers. After Wimbledon (or Mortlake) Manor passed from the Archbishop of Canterbury to the Crown in 1536, Cromwell was the first of a succession of powerful courtiers to whom it was granted, thereby acquiring authority over the village in which he had been born. Cromwell's fall and execution was engineered in 1540 by a group of conservative courtiers.

23. *Thomas Cromwell, c.1485-1540.*

Cromwell's sister Katherine married Morgan Williams, alebrewer of Putney. Their son changed his name to Cromwell out of respect for his uncle, and it was from him that Oliver Cromwell was descended.

GREAT HOUSES IN THE SEVENTEENTH CENTURY

In the late sixteenth and seventeenth centuries the older mansions were rebuilt and new ones added. In 1617 there were a dozen great houses in Putney and in 1664 two dozen, by which time about a fifth of Putney's entire population lived in these houses. In 1657 it was said that the minister of Putney might have considerable influence on the City of London 'by reason of the quality of the cittizens of greate worth and value in the said towne'.[6] Merchants who lived in Putney included Sir Thomas Lowe, Governor of the Levant Company, in 1617 and no fewer than three Lord Mayors in the later seventeenth century. Among the gentlemen were Sir William Becher, Clerk to Charles I's Privy Council, Sir William Throckmorton, Marshall of the King's Household in the 1660s, and many others. There were even a few members of the nobility: the Countess of Exeter in the 1630s and the Earl of Nottingham in the 1670s.

In 1596 John Lacy, a clothmaker, rebuilt the old Welbeck mansion in the Lower Richmond Road. Most or all of Queen Elizabeth's frequent and well-documented visits to Putney were to Lacy. She was a visitor twelve times between 1579 and 1601, usually on the way to somewhere else but sometimes for several nights.[7] By 1617 Lacy had built several other large houses on the grounds of his mansion, all with fine views of the river. In about 1600, John Parr, one of Queen Elizabeth's embroiderers, built himself a substantial house in the High Street, where Werter Road now runs. Next door was another substantial

24. *John Lacy's mansion in the Lower Richmond Road, later known as 'Putney Palace'.*

25. Essex House in Putney High Street, re-fronted in the late seventeenth or early eighteenth century (watercolour, c.1810).

26. Fairfax House in Putney High Streeet, on the site of Montserrat Road. Demolished in 1887.

house, of brick (later known as Essex House), with Queen Elizabeth's arms on several of the ceilings. (Sainsbury's supermarket stands on the garden of this house). Both Upper Place and Thomas Rich's 'chief place' were either rebuilt or extended, since both acquired galleries, a fashionable amenity of the late sixteenth and early seventeenth centuries.

Fairfax House in the High Street was built in about the 1630s by Henry White, a baker and landowner. His property passed via his daughter to the Pettiward family, who extended the house southwards and added its magnificent shell doorway, which still exists as part of a house in West Hampstead. The Pettiwards lived in Putney until about 1810, and still owned Putney property in the present century – a unique example of continuity of landownership. A much larger house was built in 1634-6 by Sir Abraham Dawes on the present site of Putney Station. By the later seventeenth century the preferred type was the tall brick house, such as Putney House, on the site of Carmalt Gardens.

Putney's largest houses in 1664, as indicated by their payments towards the tax on hearths or chimneys, were the one built by Sir Abraham Dawes (46 hearths), Coalecroft (the former Upper Place, 31), and

27. Henry White, c.1585-1658. (Re-drawn from a contemporary portrait.)

28. Sir Abraham Dawes, 1571-1640 (painting by Cornelius Janssen).

Fairfax House (20). All the twenty houses with ten or more hearths can be regarded as great houses. They were of similar size to the smaller country seats elsewhere, but were very different in purpose and character, lacking substantial grounds and probably having few grand rooms. Few had more than an acre or two of garden. Fairfax House in 1675 contained a hall, little parlour, best parlour, kitchen, dining room, five chambers, closet, little and great studies, nursery and seven garrets, and it was extended later, but when the Vestry considered buying it for public use in 1887 to save it from demolition, the parish surveyor complained of 'small, dark, low ceiling rooms'.[8] Wealth was probably displayed chiefly through the furnishings: for example, in 1684 John Parr's house, then occupied by a merchant, Peter Proby, included 'the gilt leather roome' and 'the green druggett roome', as well as many tapestries, carpets and pictures.[9]

People like Proby were seeking not country estates but houses with gardens within a short ferry, horse or coach ride from London – houses to which they could retire in the summer when the city became unpleasant; as Defoe put it, they left the 'sin and seacoal in the busy city' to enjoy the 'gay excursions' of summer.[10] Most had a house in London, and some had a country estate elsewhere. Putney in summer and winter were two very different places.

Although many of the merchants and gentlemen stayed only briefly in Putney, sometimes merely leasing a house for a few years, several families did become large landowners and took a much greater interest in the place. One who left his mark was Sir Abraham Dawes, who lived in Putney from 1620 until his death in 1640. Dawes made his fortune out of his position as a collector of the customs and invested much of it in Putney, especially in building his house. In the 1620s or 1630s he provided an almshouse 'for the perpetual habitation of twelve poor indigent, decayed and decreped almsmen and almswomen', and its nineteenth-century successor still stands in Putney Bridge Road.[11]

ROEHAMPTON

Roehampton appears not to have had any great houses at the start of the seventeenth century, and most of its landholders lived elsewhere. Its representatives on the Putney Vestry were farmers, whereas most of Putney's were merchants and gentlemen. Drastic change came suddenly in the 1620s. The man who transformed Roehampton was David Papillon, a Huguenot, who bought his first land in Roehampton in 1619. By 1622 he had built a large house later known as Elm Grove, on the site now occupied by Digby Stuart College. He sold this to George Heriot, James I's jeweller (the 'jingling Geordie' in Sir Walter Scott's *Fortunes of Nigel*). Later it passed to the Harvey family, and William Harvey, discoverer of the circulation of the blood, spent his last years there in the 1650s. By 1625 Papillon had built what became known as Roehampton Great House, whose site is

29. *The almshouse provided in Putney Bridge Road by Sir Abraham Dawes; replaced by the present building in 1861.*

now occupied by the Froebel Institute, and also a third large house east of Roehampton Lane which may have been the predecessor of Roehampton House (now part of Queen Mary's Hospital). By 1626 he had sold all his Roehampton land and left the parish, presumably much richer than when he arrived.[12]

The Great House was sold to Sir Richard Weston, Charles I's Lord Treasurer, subsequently Earl of Portland. Weston extended the house, adding a chapel and making it one of the largest houses in Surrey, with 57 hearths in 1664. He also created a large new park, called Roehampton Park, occupying most of the area from Palewell Fields to Roehampton Lane and from the Upper Richmond Road to Richmond Park. Roehampton became virtually an estate village. Weston's embellishments at Roehampton included a bronze statue of Charles I, which was removed from Roehampton in 1644,[13] narrowly escaped being melted down by the Parliamentarians and now stands at the top of Whitehall. The Great House was later occupied by a succession of illustrious owners, notably from 1648 until her death in 1675 the Dowager Countess of Devonshire, who made it a centre for Royalist intrigue prior to the Restoration in 1660 and subsequently received a number of visits from Charles II. Unfortunately no illustrations are known of the Great House or Papillon's other Roehampton houses.

Almost every other part of Roehampton also changed in the 1630s. Charles I created Richmond Park, swallowing up several hundred acres of Roehampton farmland. Putney Park had been retained by the Crown when it disposed of Wimbledon

30. *David Papillon, 1581-1659.*

Manor, presumably because a deer park in the area was useful both for recreation and for provisioning royal palaces. James I, for example, was said to be 'constantly resorting to the said Parke for his pleasure' in the early seventeenth century.[14] In 1626 Charles I sold it, and in 1636 Sir Abraham Dawes converted it from a deer park to arable and pasture fields. The lodge became a great house. Putney Park Lane, first recorded in 1725, was its private avenue to the Heath and was only later extended northwards to the Upper Richmond Road.[15]

Papillon's activities gave a considerable boost to Roehampton, and by 1664 there were 59 households, twice as many as in 1617, containing perhaps 350 people. During this period much of what we know as Roehampton High Street became built up, entirely on former common land. Only later, during the eighteenth century, did the old village in Roehampton Lane finally disappear, as its sites were taken for new mansions, and the new village then came to be regarded as *the* Roehampton village. One of the new mansions was Roehampton House, which was built in 1710-12 by Thomas Archer for Thomas Cary, a London merchant.

32. *Richard Weston, Earl of Portland, 1577-1635.*

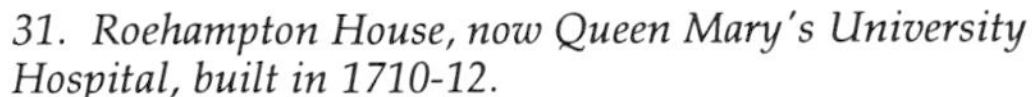

31. *Roehampton House, now Queen Mary's University Hospital, built in 1710-12.*

A Prosperous Community

With so many fine houses and well-to-do inhabitants, Putney in the seventeenth century was a prosperous community. A manorial survey of 1617[1] and Nicholas Lane's map of 1636 provide the first really detailed picture of it. They indicate a large village strung out along the full length of the High Street, with buildings packed most closely together near the river. Where the High Street reached the riverside were the village's most important buildings: the church, the Red Lion (the main inn) and other inns such as the White Lion. Here also was the ferry landing, and with watermen seeking passengers and people embarking and disembarking it must have been a bustling place. A little way up the High Street, at the junction with Putney Bridge Road, were the stocks for punishing wrongdoers.[2]

Further from the river, the houses in the High Street tended to be larger, including mansions and farmhouses, and mingled with gardens, orchards and barns. As for the road itself, until the parish had it paved at great expense in 1656 it was famous for 'deep and dangerous mires' which periodically trapped coaches and carts in winter. At the junction of the High Street and the Upper Richmond Road was the pound for confining stray animals. There were several farms on Putney Hill, and at the top the Upper Heath Gate, which prevented animals wandering off the Common. South of this the only structure was a recently-built windmill by the Portsmouth Road (not the present Wimbledon Common Windmill, which is further south). By 1636 the windmill had been joined by a bowling green (on the site of Heathview Gardens). There were also buildings by the river, including the brewhouse in Brewhouse Lane and, further west, John Lacy's mansion. The increasing influence of London was indicated by the new mansions, the spread of market gardening and the growing traffic by river and road.

Putney was growing faster than at any time in its history prior to the nineteenth century. The 106 dwellings in 1617 suggest a population of about 600, and in 1664, less than 50 years later, the number of dwellings had almost doubled.[3] The 1617 survey shows some of the ways this was happening: on the northern corner of Felsham Road and the High Street, for example, was a row of eight little cottages built in the grounds of a farmhouse, and elsewhere farms and cottages had been subdivided. However, there had been virtually no expansion of the built-up area between 1497 and 1617. Until the open fields were enclosed and the right of manorial tenants to graze

33. Frontispiece of a pamphlet about the murder of the miller at Putney's windmill in 1614. According to the pamphleteer, the miller's 'naturall inclination was to bee sparing and in a manner miserable in his howse-keeping, which procured him the hatred of his servants and familie'.

A Horrible Creuel and bloudy Murther,
Committed at Putney in Surrey on the 21. of
Aprill laſt, 1614, being thurſday, vpon the body
of Edward Hall *a Miller of the ſame pariſh,*
Done by the hands of *Iohn Selling, Peeter Pet* and *Edward Streater,*
his ſeruants to the ſaid *Hall*, each of them giuing
him a deadly blow (as he lay ſleeping)
with a Pickax.

Publiſhed by Authority.

Imprinted at London for *Iohn Wright*, and are to be ſold without Newgate at the ſigne of the Bible. 1614.

34. Looking west along the Lower Richmond Road from its junction with Putney High Street, c.1880. The white buildings on the left with overhanging upper storeys were probably sixteenth-century.

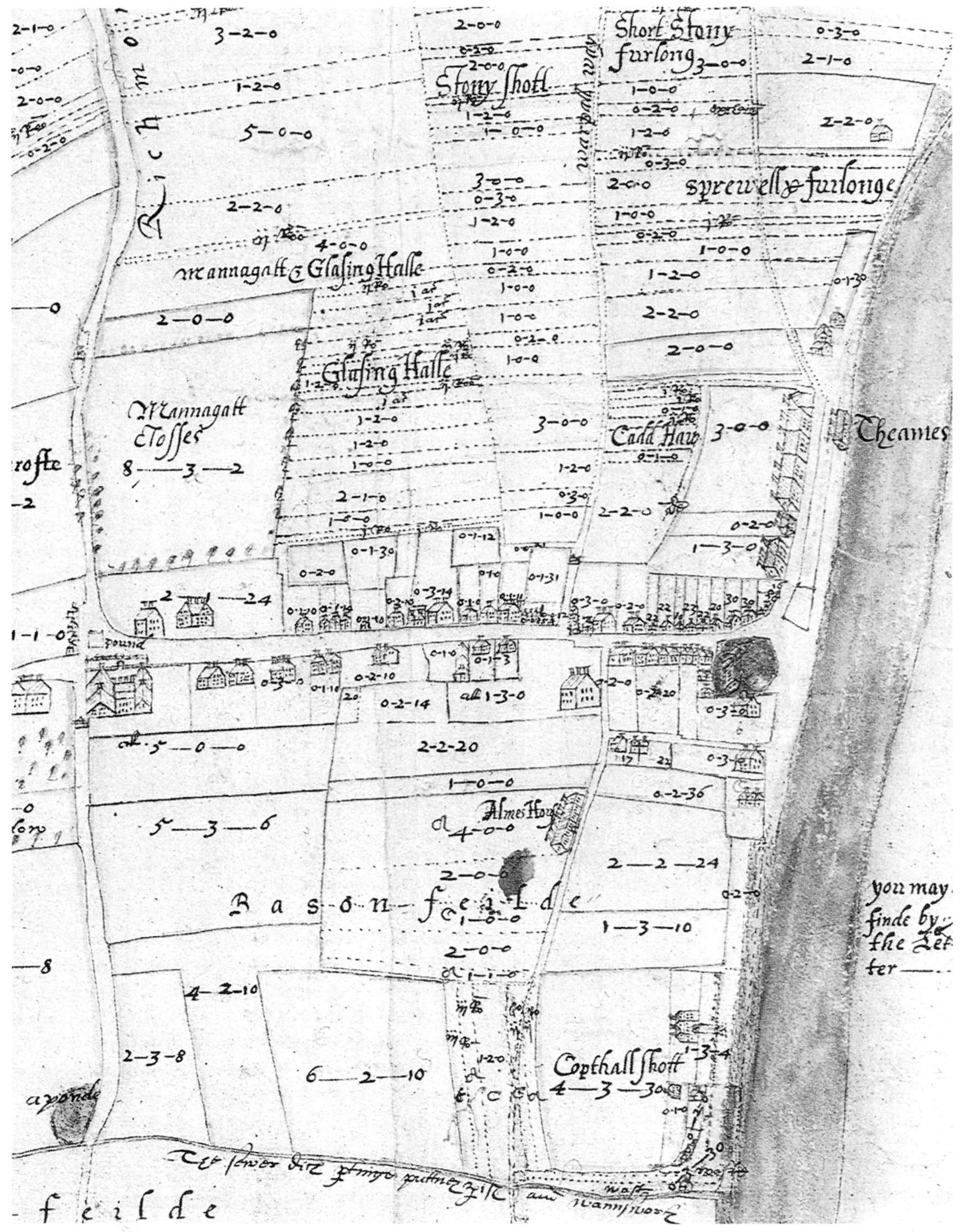

35. *The Putney High Street area on Nicholas Lane's map of Putney in 1636. North is to the right. The dark patch at one end of Putney High Street was the church. The very large house at the other end, by the pound, was Sir Abraham Dawes' house.*

36. Houses on the east side of Putney High Street near St Mary's Church, probably dating from the seventeenth century. W. (William) Field was a photographer who took many of the photographs used in this book.

37. Sixteenth or seventeenth-century buildings in Putney High Street between St Mary's Church and Putney Bridge Road.

animals on them was extinguished, they could not be built on. There was never a formal enclosure in Putney, but in the mid-seventeenth century much of the more fertile land was enclosed for market gardening, and thereafter buildings began to appear in significant numbers away from the High Street, chiefly in the Lower Richmond Road but including a scatter of farmhouses and mansions elsewhere.[4] Putney's growth between the 1660s and the next list of households in 1736 was slower than before (up from about 200 to 290, indicating a population of about 1800 in 1736),[5] but may have had a greater impact on its appearance, with the spread of building to new sites and greater use of brick and tile in place of wood and thatch.

The first useful description of Putney's housing is given by the records of the hearth tax in the 1660s, which can be combined with information from probate inventories listing people's possessions room by room after their death. The commonest form of house in both Putney and Roehampton then consisted of kitchen and parlour on the ground floor, two chambers over them, and sometimes garrets above. The degree of comfort in such houses varied: the two-hearth houses, accounting for 41% of the parish's total, had fires in kitchen and parlour, and were occupied by some of the more substantial tradesmen as well as by people too poor to pay the tax. Some of the one-hearth houses (22% of the total) were smaller: sometimes just two rooms, and no doubt sometimes

38. Houses on the east side of Putney High Street, a little north of the present Montserrat Road. Putney's tithe barn stood at the back of a yard to their left. The left-hand house appears to be eighteenth-century; that on the right seventeenth-century. Demolished about 1880.

a single room. An example recorded in about 1720 is a cottage on Putney Hill nicknamed Bears Den Hall, with just a ground floor room and an upper room, the latter reached by a ladder and being open to the thatched roof.[6] The poorest people of all tended to live in a single room rented for them by the parish or allocated to them in the almshouse. Most new housing was provided piecemeal, and probably the largest developer in seventeenth-century Putney was George Platt, a waterman, whose wife inherited a small landholding in about 1660. By the end of the century, Platt had divided the Queens Head Inn into nine dwellings and had built ten small houses on a site in Felsham Road.

39. (Left) Two late seventeenth-century houses on the west side of Putney High Street, a little south of Lacy Road, drawn in 1899.

40. (Below) Chatfield House, two houses of about 1700 on the west side of Putney High Street opposite Montserrat Road, drawn in 1887. Though rebuilt, the facade of the house, minus the wings, was copied in the present building on the site.

FARMERS, WATERMEN AND INNKEEPERS

How did the people of Putney make a living?[7] First, there was employment generated by the occupants of the great houses, either directly (about 10% of the population in the 1660s were servants in the great houses) or indirectly, through their patronage of tradesmen like Henry Tunstall the glazier and Edward Jones the locksmith.

Secondly, there was farming. This, however, was less important than might have been expected: only about a fifth of the householders working in Putney gained their living directly from it, though others relied on it indirectly, such as the blacksmith and the miller, or assisted in the fields at harvest time. From the 1640s much of the best land was used for market gardening and orchards. Poultry farming was also important, and in the 1660s the farmers, market gardeners and poulterers were mostly among the parish's wealthier inhabitants.

The third major source of employment was transport, especially water transport. In the 1660s no fewer than 40% of the householders working in Putney (a third of *all* householders) were watermen, making their living from the cross-river ferry, the long-haul ferry to London, goods traffic and fishing. The watermen were almost all poor, and they also suffered from press gangs: at least 14 Putney watermen died at sea in His Majesty's service in the 1690s. Of all Putney's inhabitants, however, they were the least dependent on the occupants of the great houses, and consequently such little political or religious radicalism as there was in Putney was to be found among them. For example, the most prominent of the small group of Putney Quakers during Charles II's reign was a waterman, Richard Broughton, who kept an alehouse near the church called the Watermen's Arms.

Road transport was also important, particularly in providing custom for the inns, of which the Red Lion, the White Lion and the Bull, next to each other opposite the ferry landing, were the most important. There was considerable traffic through Putney, so much so that in 1671 and again in 1688 it was proposed (unsuccessfully) to build a bridge, which would have been the only one between Kingston and London. Numerous 'wandring poor people', soldiers, sailors and 'great bellied women' appear in the churchwardens' accounts as recipients of charity, as well as more exotic characters such as 'a French frire turned a Protestant' (1633), an Irish gentlewoman who had had 21 children (1635) and '3 poor gent that had been slaves in Barbadoes' (1660).

Fourthly, although Putney has never had much industry, a surprising number of industries has operated there at different times. The longest lasting was brewing, but there was also the manufacture of soap ash (a sort of fertilizer) in the 1630s, a pottery from about 1668 to 1739 (on the site of Glendarvon Street), and distilling in the 1680s. In 1625 one of the inhabitants was 'Edward Addams silkeman', and the mulberry trees he would have needed for his trade may have been the basis of the legend that Oliver Cromwell used the time he spent in Putney to plant mulberry trees.

One other source of employment was Putney's schools, attracting children of the well-to-do from a wide area. In 1649, for example, John Evelyn visited Putney 'to see the schooles and colledges of the young gentlewomen', and in April 1667 Samuel Pepys came by boat to Putney Church, 'where I saw the girls of the schools, few of which pretty'. They were not even alluring enough to keep him awake during the sermon, as a result of which he lost his hat through a hole under the pulpit. Putney was a good location for schools because of its fashionable character and because its air was considered particularly healthy.[8] The most important of them was Henry Portman's school 'for the education and breedinge upp of younge gentlewomen and for teachinge of them their needle and other things fitt for them to learne'. This was in existence by 1638 (on the site now occupied by the ICL block), moved to one of the houses on the Kenilworth Court site in about 1663, and continued until 1702. Portman claimed he employed twenty servants and teachers, and boasted of having 'lords', knights' and gentlemen's daughters of good repute and esteeme' as scholars. In the 1650s there was a boys' school run by Noah Bridges, a renowned mathematician and expert on shorthand, who had been Clerk to the Parliament which sat at Oxford during the Civil War.[9]

Many families earned extra income by looking after nurse children from London, sent to Putney either for wet nursing or simply for healthy air. About 40% of Putney's households had them in the 1650s and 1660s, and the most characteristic sound in Putney must

41. House by the Thames east of St Mary's Church, in which Henry Portman carried on his school for young ladies from the 1630s to about 1663.

42. *Noah Bridges.*

have been the crying of children. The nurse children undoubtedly safeguarded many Putney families from poverty.

COMMUNITY AND GOVERNMENT

The inhabitants of the great houses dominated Putney in several ways: as owners of most of the land and dwellings, as employers of many of the inhabitants, and through their control of the parish Vestry, an increasingly powerful body in the seventeenth century, with its own meeting house on the north side of the church from 1629. The Vestry's tasks were maintenance of the church, allocation of pews (a controversial matter), distribution of poor relief and, in fact, dealing with almost any matter which affected the parish.

However, the most significant divide within Putney was not between gentlemen and others but between the substantial tradesmen and farmers and those below them. The more substantial were the sort of people who purchased the right to their own pew in the church and who occasionally filled one of the manorial or parochial offices, such as overseer of the poor. About half of Putney's inhabitants were below this crucial divide and played little part in the public life of the parish. Few of these were actually destitute and dependent on the parish, but most would have needed poor relief when they became old or fell ill. The Vestry took good care to minimise its liabilities towards both inhabitants and travellers, even (in 1711) paying one shilling to 'a waterman looking [after] a drowned man and keeping him from shore', to save the cost of a pauper burial.[10] However, judging by the proportion of householders exempted from taxation on grounds of poverty in 1664 (23%), poverty was less widespread in Putney Parish than in the country as a whole. The numbers dependent on poor relief or in the almshouses reached a low point of about 3% in Putney in the 1670s.

The effectiveness of Putney's Vestry was tested most severely during times of plague. During Elizabeth's reign Putney seems to have been sufficiently far from London not to be affected. On several occasions the scholars and choristers of Westminster School were evacuated to Putney, as in 1567, when they acted a play there.[11] In the seventeenth century, on the other hand, there were 26 plague deaths at Putney in 1625-6 and 87 (about 7% of the population) in 1665-7; there were also a few deaths most years from 1636 to 1647. In both major outbreaks watermen were the first victims, which suggests how the disease was brought from London. Pesthouses to confine infected people were put up on four occasions – usually a couple of wooden huts, taken down again when the danger had passed. In 1665 and possibly the other years they were on the edge of the Lower Common, opposite the present Putney Hospital. The pesthouses of 1665 were built of brick and were retained as cheap accommodation; they apparently survived until 1860, when they were replaced by Nos. 24-29 Commondale.

THE CIVIL WARS AND INTERREGNUM

Putney briefly attained national prominence during the Civil Wars. War first impinged on Putney in November 1642, shortly after the stand-off between the two armies at Turnham Green, when the King was prevented from marching on London. The Earl of Essex, commander of the parliamentary forces, built a bridge of boats guarded by forts at Putney so as to be able to confront the King if he crossed the Thames by Kingston Bridge. It was probably just outside the parish, at the west end of what is now Wandsworth Park, although the exact site is uncertain.[12] However, the King instead retreated to Oxford and the boats must soon have been reclaimed by their owners. The earthworks on the Putney side were still visible in the nineteenth century.

From 27 August to 13 November 1647 the New Model Army's headquarters was at Putney, which suddenly became the centre of effective political power. The Army placed itself between Parliament and the City on the one hand and King Charles imprisoned at Hampton Court on the other. Officers and ordinary soldiers were billeted on the inhabitants. During this period (28 October to 5 November)

43. A meeting of the New Model Army's Council in 1647.

44. Colonel Thomas Rainborough, one of the leading radicals at the Putney Debates. He made the famous observation that 'the poorest he that is in England hath a life to live as the greatest he', and therefore that government should be by consent. Killed during a kidnap attempt by Royalists in 1648.

occurred the famous 'Putney Debates', when army officers and the more radical representatives of the rank and file met around the communion table in Putney Church to consider the country's future government. Although ideas such as that 'a man is not bound to a system of government which he hath not had any hand in setting over him' did not carry the day, these ideas have reverberated through the centuries since.

The Civil Wars had more local aspects too, ranging from the marriage of four local girls to soldiers stationed in Richmond Park in the 1650s to punitive measures against people who had benefited from Charles I's favour. The chief casualties were the Dawes family, who by 1640 had held the greater part of the land in both Putney and Roehampton. Fines and imprisonment forced them to disgorge many of their possessions and they became just one among many gentry families in Putney.

Clergymen also came under close scrutiny, and Putney had two, and very nearly three, curates ejected: one for belonging to the catholicizing tendency favoured by Charles I and another who was Presbyterian but Royalist. The third, Christopher Hudson, a moderate puritan, ran into trouble, probably for excessive moderation, in 1657. A successor was actually appointed, but the people of Putney clearly preferred Hudson, as they had to be ordered to allow the new curate 'quietly to preach'. Hudson not only survived this episode but was confirmed in his post after the Restoration.

Several local customs fell victim to the new regime of the 1640s and 1650s, including the annual perambulation. Each year the boys had beaten the bounds of the parish, with refreshments of bread, cheese and beer at suitable points en route, and there had been a dinner for the entire parish at the Red Lion. The practice was revived at the Restoration, but the dinner succumbed to the even deadlier enemy of expenditure cuts once the total cost started to exceed £5.

45. Old Putney Bridge in 1886, looking towards Fulham and showing the massive timber supports.

Bridge and Town

THE BRIDGE

In the seventeenth century and earlier, Putney's inhabitants could reach London either by road or by water. The occupants of the great houses had their own coaches and coachmen; Roger Pettiward of Fairfax House, for example, had two coach horses and 'a charriot' in 1675. But the river may have been the usual way of reaching London and Westminster, since journeys by road involved either the time-consuming ferry-crossing or going round by London Bridge. Some gentlemen, like Sir Thomas Dawes in 1648, referred in their wills to 'my waterman', which suggests that their use of the river was frequent.[1]

In 1725, admittedly when trying to make the case for a bridge, witnesses before a parliamentary committee stressed the danger and inconvenience of the ferry: the ferry boats were sometimes driven down the river as far as Wandsworth in stormy weather, three passengers had drowned a few months previously, there was sometimes a half-hour wait (very damaging to horses), and 'sometimes the coaches can't get over at all'.[2]

Any would-be bridge builders faced not only heavy costs but also the opposition of vested interests, particularly the watermen and the City of London, but as traffic increased a bridge became increasingly necessary. The passing of the Act for Putney's first bridge (known as Fulham Bridge) in 1726 owed much to the support of Sir Robert Walpole, Britain's first Prime Minister, who, it was said, had once been kept waiting by politically-motivated ferrymen when he was in a hurry to cross. Putney may have been chosen as the site rather than Westminster or Lambeth because it was less likely to arouse the City of London's opposition.

The bridge opened in 1729. It was built of wood and was 786 feet long and 23 feet wide (19 feet for the carriageway and 4 feet for a footpath on the east side). In order that it could connect Fulham and Putney High Streets without having a lengthy diagonal course, the approach road curved around the north side of Putney churchyard. There was a small brick toll-house on the Putney side, against the churchyard wall, and a larger one on the Fulham side astride the roadway, in which the proprietors held meetings.

As the bridge had been built at heavy cost (£23,973) by a private company, tolls had to be charged to give them a return on their money. They ranged from ½d for a foot passenger (1d on Sundays) to 2/- for a six-horse coach. Twenty cattle could cross for 12d. The surviving toll books give an idea of the sort of traffic; on 8 February 1740, for example, there were 12 six-

46. Photograph taken from the tower of St Mary's Church, c.1878, looking towards Fulham, showing the aqueduct on the left and the bridge on the right.

horse coaches, three four-horse coaches, 24 coaches with less than four horses, 334 horses, mules and asses, 15 hogs and 1052 foot-passengers. Although rebuilding was occasionally contemplated, the wooden structure remained in service for just over 150 years, the only structural alteration being the replacement of the three central spans with an iron section in 1871 to provide a wider passage for vessels.[3]

Several road improvements were made at about the time the bridge was built, particularly by turnpike trusts, which were authorised to take tolls from users of their stretch of road and spend them on repairing and improving the road. The Southwark to Kingston road, which passed up West Hill and across Putney Heath, was turnpiked in 1718, and several roads in Kensington, Chelsea and Fulham in 1726. Queens Ride across the Lower Common was considerably improved in 1736-40, probably at the instigation of Queen Caroline (wife of George II) to improve the access to Richmond Park.[4]

The bridge and the improved roads must have encouraged Putney's gentlemen and merchants to use their carriages more for journeys to London and Westminster, instead of going by boat. There was also an increasing number of regular stage coach services. By 1681 stage coaches to London were available from Fulham, but only once a day. By the 1740s there were a number of coach services crossing the bridge, and in 1801 Putney had a coach business of its own: Mr Rix's stage coaches offered 11 services a day from Putney to the City, starting at 7 am. His yard was in Wellington Place, approached through an arch just south of the White Lion. Putney also benefited both from coaches passing through to Richmond and elsewhere and from those which stopped just over the river in Fulham (saving the bridge toll). Consequently it had one of the best services of any suburb south of the river. In 1825, there were no services from the City terminating at Putney, but 28 a day to Fulham, 12 to Richmond, two to Wimbledon and one to Roehampton. However, these services were slow (almost an hour to Putney) and expensive, and would not have been very convenient for daily commuting.[5]

The bridge tolls indicate the continuing growth of road traffic. Despite unchanged charges and the opening of new bridges (such as Battersea in 1773), toll income rose from £2,455 a year in the 1760s to a peak of £6,676 a year in the 1810s.[6] Road improvements continued to be made: in 1830, for example, Putney's major roads were 'macadamised', that is, surfaced with small angular stones, which made it easier for horses to draw vehicles.[7] Road vehicles were improved too.

47. The toll collector on the Putney side, 1880.

48. St Mary's Church and the approach to the bridge (watercolour, c.1780).

NEW BUILDINGS

Apart from the bridge, the parish experienced three significant changes in the eighteenth century: the establishment of a workhouse in about 1726, the proliferation of luxurious villas beside Putney Heath and at Roehampton from the 1750s (discussed in the next chapter), and the construction of a towpath beside the Thames in 1776-7. The workhouse, which existed for just over a century, stood near the bottom of the High Street, at the end of what is now Weimar Street, and usually contained thirty to fifty of Putney's poorest inhabitants. From 1729, any paupers seeking pensions from the parish were to be placed in the workhouse; they were also required to wear pauper badges. As elsewhere, the workhouse was an expensive failure: there was great difficulty finding anyone competent and honest to run it, it was subject to profiteering by local firms, and the work done failed to produce significant income. It seems to have been at its worst and most overcrowded in about 1820, when, according to Dr Carmalt, who subsequently reformed it, it was 'crowded almost to suffocation with paupers of all ages and characters... a scene of the most complete disorder and insubordination, poor hygiene, no attempt at employment... idleness, profligacy and improvidence had been surer passports than age or infirmity to this castle of indolence'. Disappointingly for Dr Carmalt, the inhabitants 'seemed to manifest an appearance of perfect satisfaction and enjoyment'. In 1836 the Putney paupers were moved to the Union Workhouse on East Hill.[8]

Creation of the towpath, which headed westwards from the foot of the High Street, meant that for the first time it was possible to walk along a substantial part of Putney's foreshore, and the sight of horses hauling barges must have become familiar.[9]

The parish's population grew only slowly in the eighteenth century, from about 2000 in 1736 to 2428 in 1801.[10] The number of houses increased, especially along the Lower Richmond Road, but there were no really large housing developments and there was no drastic change in the shape of Putney's built-up area, apart from a few new patches of working class housing. Except for the Heath and Roehampton, Putney High Street remained the best address in the parish. The largest development of small houses in the eighteenth century was Biggs Row (behind the Half Moon), which was later joined by other small terraces and housed Putney's Irish community in the mid-nine-

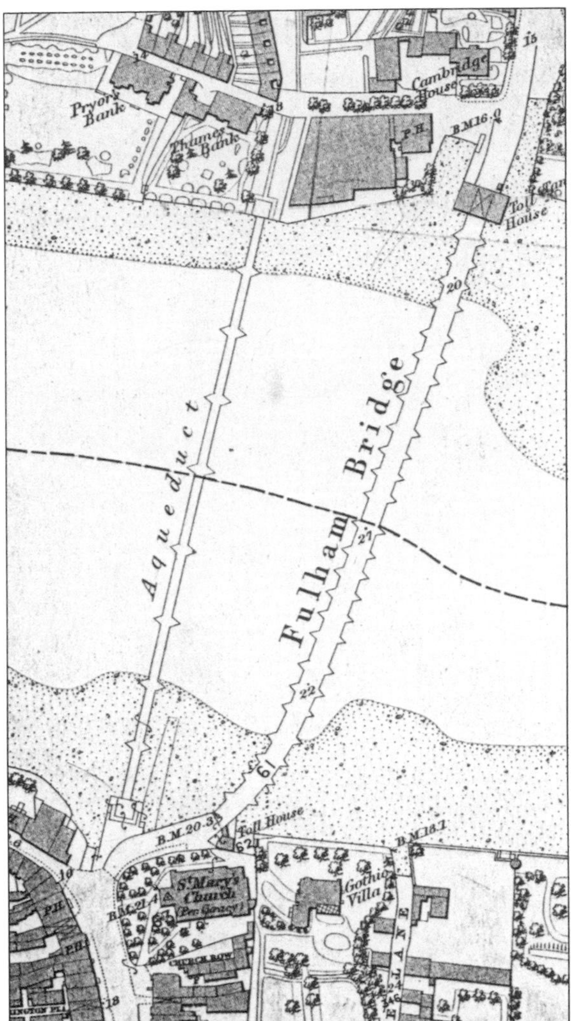

49. *Bridge and aqueduct in 1865, showing the awkward approach to Putney High Street from the bridge. The aqueduct is on the line of the present bridge.*

FREEHOLD SHARES

IN

FULHAM AND PUTNEY BRIDGE,

ENTITLING THE PROPRIETORS TO

VOTES FOR MIDDLESEX AND EAST SURREY.

Particulars and Conditions of Sale

OF

Three-Fourth Parts & Four-Twentieth Parts

OF

A SHARE

IN

FULHAM & PUTNEY BRIDGE,

ENTITLING THE PROPRIETORS TO

VOTES FOR MIDDLESEX & EAST SURREY;

Which will be Sold by Auction,

BY MESSRS.

VENTOM & HUGHES,

AT THE AUCTION MART,

NEAR THE BANK,

On THURSDAY, the 28th Day of APRIL, 1842,

50. *Advertisement for a sale of shares in the bridge. The shares counted as freehold property and carried the right to vote in parliamentary elections in two counties.*

teenth century. Several smaller developments, such as Wickham's Rents (just west of Walkers Place in Felsham Road), included a few back-to-backs, which were unusual in the London area. Other small houses - usually just short terraces or alleys - were built around the Lower Common, the Platt, the northern end of Quill Lane, Brewhouse Lane and in alleys leading off the High Street. The apparently random distribution of working class housing developments prior to the nineteenth century seems to reflect the fact that they were built on whatever land happened to be owned by the smaller, less genteel landowners, perhaps because such developments were only profitable if the owner was willing to put considerable effort into collecting rents. By the early nineteenth century even the smallest new houses were of brick, though a few timber cottages were still being built in Roehampton.[11] There was also greater use of tiles, and pantiles can still be seen on most of the surviving old buildings, such as the Montague Arms in Roehampton.

Rapid growth resumed in the early nineteenth century, and the parish's population rose between 1801 and 1831 from 2428 to 3811. Gay Street and River Street, laid out on part of the Putney Palace site in 1826, indicated the shape of things to come. They consisted eventually of 78 brick dwellings, nearly all of four rooms. It was both the first time one of Putney's great houses had been demolished for development and also the first time a significant number of new houses (albeit of very poor quality) had been set out in a new street.

51. Putney seen from the bridge in about 1750, before the construction of the towpath. Three inns or alehouses can be seen: the Red Lion, the Eight Bells and the Star and Garter, of which only the last survives.

52. The Star and Garter and the towpath, c.1840.

53. Looking west along the Lower Richmond Road, c.1880. On the left is the Terrace, built about 1800 and now replaced by Kenilworth Court.

54. The bridge and foreshore in 1792.

55. The towpath bridge over Beverley Brook, with a horse towing a barge on the Thames (lithograph, c.1820).

56. Henry's Place, an alley off Brewhouse Lane (lithograph, 1815).

57. John Rocque's map of the area around London, surveyed in 1740-5. Prominent features include Edward Gibbon's estate east of Putney Hill, the avenue known as Putney Park Lane, the bowling green on the Heath, Roehampton House and Roehampton Great House (since replaced by Grove House) with its large formal garden.

58. *Biggs Row, looking north towards the Lower Richmond Road, c.1905.*

59. *The junction of River Street and Gay Street, c.1955.*

60. Morrison's Farm, by the Lower Common near All Saints Church, c.1880.

61. 'Cottages near Roehampton', not yet identified but possibly in Putney Vale (watercolour by Revd James Bourne, early nineteenth century).

62. A farm on the site of Holroyd Road, seen from the southern end of Parkfields.

63. The town of Putney in 1787.

EARNING A LIVING

The occupations recorded in Putney in 1664 can be compared with those given in the 1851 census. There were greatly increased numbers of nearly every occupation, but the proportions were not greatly altered. The higher classes (not easy to define but including gentlemen, merchants and professional people) formed roughly 15 to 20% at both dates. Most of these are likely to have worked in London (if they worked at all), but daily commuters were probably rare among them until after the railway opened in 1846.

Of those working in Putney itself, the one big change was the decline of the watermen. Their number fell by half, and their percentage of all householders declined from about 31% to 4%. This probably resulted less from the replacement of the ferry than from the general rise of road transport at the expense of river transport. The watermen also claimed in the early 1840s to have been hard-hit by the new steamboats plying between Richmond, Putney and London.[12] One of the 23 watermen in 1851 was a fisherman, and even in 1891 there was still a fisherman living in Spring Passage.

Other changes were an increased proportion in the building trades (14% compared with 6%), in road transport (8% compared with about 2%, including coachmen, carmen, horsekeepers and an omnibus conductor), and in miscellaneous trades which had mostly not existed in 1664 or had been combined with other occupations (16% compared with 6%). By 1851 Putney had a bookseller, a pawnbroker and auctioneer and several printers and stationers, for example. As these figures relate only to heads of households, they take no account of domestic servants, who formed 12% of the parish's total population in 1851.[13]

Putney lacked much industry at either date: in 1851 the only large-scale industries were Wood's Anchor Brewery, just off the High Street south of Felsham Road, and Dallett's soap works, almost on the corner of Putney Bridge Road and the High Street. There were however many smaller-scale crafts, such as boatbuilding.

Agriculture, perhaps surprisingly, employed about five times as many householders in 1851 as in 1664, and almost the same percentage (16% compared with 14%). The probable reason is that only a small proportion of the land had yet been built on, and what remained was worked much more intensively, especially by gardeners and market gardeners, who formed the second largest occupational group in Putney in 1851, after the labourers. The market garden ground was certainly minutely tended. An inventory of 1750 of the fields of William Charlwood, whose house was on the site of the Quill, records 37 different plants on his several dozen acres, including asparagus, strawberries, tulips, and garlic. Most of this was destined for Covent Garden market, where he had a stand.[14]

Some people, of course, resided in Putney for enjoyment rather than work, including two highly eccentric characters who occupied a cottage on Putney Hill (probably in the Kersfield Road area) in the years up to 1720. They were Humphrey Skelton, an upholsterer, 'a facetious and whimsical man', and Charles Christian Reisen, a famous engraver of gems, 'who was also an odd creature, & being a rough sort of man was called *the Bear* - they were both humorous fellows & always snarling at one another'. In the cottage, which became known as Bears Den Hall, 'they lived without any servant or cookery. They had only a dog. They went up a ladder to a bedchamber, where there was only one bed, which served them both, & a small window where the head could hardly pass – thatched and no cieling. The ground floor...was entirely free from chairs and benches. They lived there only in summer, & generally walked together. A club of artists and painters used to go there to have a little fun in summer'.[15]

64. *Bears Den Hall on Putney Hill, an example of Putney's poorest housing, used in the early eighteenth century as a summer house by Humphrey Skelton and Charles Christian Reisen. Demolished c.1720. (Engraving by George Vertue.)*

Villas and Mansions

The second half of the eighteenth century was the main period for building villas in Putney and Roehampton, especially the latter. The aim was to acquire, not large, sprawling mansions, but elegant houses of moderate size in beautiful grounds where a pleasant country life could be lived in summer in distinguished company within easy reach of London. The attractions of Roehampton appear to have been its exclusivity, its elevated situation with fine views over the Thames valley, and amenities such as Putney Heath and Richmond Park. Lysons emphasised 'the beauties of the surrounding scenery and the contiguity to Richmond Park'. George Clive, for whom Mount Clare was built, stated in 1775 that he had left it in his will to his wife, 'for her pleasure and the health of my children are the motives for laying out so much money'.[1]

The villa period begins in the 1750s with the houses north of Putney Heath – from east to west, Ripon House, Grantham House, Ashburton House, Exeter House and Gifford House, followed by Dover House in 1764. Lord Bessborough's Parksted (now called Manresa House) was built in the early 1760s, surrounded by a new park known (confusingly) as Roehampton Park and now occupied by the Alton East Estate. The earlier Roehampton Park surrounding the Great House was broken up between 1770 and 1786. Several new villas were built there (Mount Clare, Templeton, Clarence Lodge and Lower Grove House) and Downshire House and the Cedars were able to expand their grounds. There were several new houses on the Heath itself: the Bowling Green House was converted to a private house in about 1770 and David Hartley's Fireproof House (later known as Wildcroft) was built in 1776. Hartley's house incorporated his invention of fireproof sheets of iron or copper placed between floors and was demonstrated there by lighting a fire underneath a room in which King George III and his Queen were having breakfast; it is commemorated by an obelisk near Tibbets Corner. Bristol House probably dated from about the

65. Mount Clare, 1784.

66. Dover House in the early nineteenth century.

67. David Hartley's Fireproof House and the obelisk commemorating his invention (see page 49). In the background is the shutter telegraph, one of a chain which conveyed messages between London and Portsmouth from 1796 to 1816. Subsequently the same site was used for a semaphore telegraph station from 1822 to 1847.

68. Lower Park, of c.1800, on Putney Hill opposite Lytton Grove. It survives, having been converted to flats in the 1930s.

69. (Above) Manresa House (then Bessborough House), c.1820.

70. (Top right) House facing the Heath immediately east of Bristol House, 1823. It was then occupied by Charles Bicknell, Solicitor to the Admiralty and father-in-law of the painter, John Constable, who was a frequent visitor there. Demolished c.1900.

71. (Bottom right) Granard Lodge, built about 1770 and demolished in 1936 (watercolour, c.1820). Granard School now stands on the site.

72. *Downshire House, c.1820.*

same time. Less favoured areas on lower ground did not attract villas until slightly later, for example the Priory and the houses east of Roehampton Lane and west of Putney Hill. By the end of the eighteenth century there was hardly a square inch in Roehampton not occupied by a villa and its grounds.[2]

As for the older houses, Sir Joshua Vanneck replaced Roehampton Great House with the more manageable Grove House in the late 1780s, the first Elm Grove burnt down in 1795, Downshire House was rebuilt in about 1770, and the present Putney Park House replaced its predecessor in about 1826.[3] Of the houses built before 1750 in the southern part of the parish, only Roehampton House has survived.

Most of the important eighteenth and early nineteenth-century architects did some work at Roehampton. Apart from Thomas Archer, already mentioned, James Gibbs, architect of St Martin in the Fields, added a room to the original Elm Grove in about 1730; Sir William Chambers, architect of Somerset House, designed Manresa House in about 1760; in the early 1770s Robert Taylor designed Mount Clare, to which an Italian architect, Placido Columbani, later added a portico; James Wyatt built Grove House in the late 1780s; Sir John Soane, architect of the Bank of England, enlarged the Cedars in 1804-7; and Sir Robert Smirke rebuilt North House (on Putney Hill) in 1828.[4] Some of these houses were in a Palladian or classical style; others, such as Downshire House and Templeton, were much plainer. The Priory was in the Gothick style popularised at Strawberry Hill. Famous landscapers were employed too, notably Capability Brown in the grounds of Mount Clare.

The spread of villas made Roehampton one of the most aristocratic neighbourhoods anywhere in the country. In 1807, the Minister of Putney noted that the families of rank in the parish were those of the Archbishop of York, the Marchioness of Downshire, Earl of Bessborough, Earl of Bristol, Lady Grantham, Lady Lucas, Lady Langham and Earl of Buckinghamshire (all of whom except the Archbishop had houses in Roehampton or beside the Heath). He added that 'besides these there are a great number of families of much respectability & wealth, who have summer residences in various parts of the parish'.[5] The Duke of Clarence (later William IV) owned Clarence Lodge in 1790-1, a period which saw the beginning of his relationship with Dorothy Jordan, an actress, who was to bear him ten children during the 20 years they lived together.[6] Several prime ministers occupied houses in Roehampton: Pitt the Younger at several different houses (he died at Bowling Green House in 1806); the Earl of Liverpool (while Lord Hawkesbury) at Dover House in 1801; Viscount Goderich (Prime Minister briefly and unsatisfactorily in 1827-8) at Ripon House from about 1832 to 1855; and the Earl of Derby at Granard Lodge in the 1860s.[7] The members of the nobility who maintained residences longest in

73. The Cedars, by the Thames on the eastern edge of Putney Parish.

74. Sir Joshua Vanneck and his family in the garden of Putney House, with the bridge and St Mary's tower in the background, painted by Arthur Devis in 1752.

Roehampton were the Earls of Bessborough at what is now Manresa House (1761-1836), the Countess de Grey and subsequently the Earl and Countess of Ripon at Ripon House (1792-1866), the Marquis of Bristol at Bristol House (1802-58), Earl Clifden at Dover House (1811-31), and the Earls of Leven and Melville at Roehampton House (1860-1910).

Bankers were always prominent at Roehampton, such as the financier Benjamin Goldsmid at Elm Grove from 1797 to 1808. In about 1800 it was said of Goldsmid's house that 'many of the first, and some of the best characters of the present day, among whom may be included Ministers, and foreigners of the highest distinction, are in the habit [of] partaking of the pleasures of this elegant mansion, nor has royalty itself deemed it beneath its notice'.[8] Lawyers were numerous too, such as Lord Robert Gifford at Gifford House (1824-6), the Attorney General who led the prosecution of Queen Caroline. Other notable residents included the naval commander, Lord Howe at Ashburton House in 1764-5; James Macpherson, discoverer and translator of the Gaelic Ossian poems (later found to be forgeries) at Gifford House in 1774-96; an Archbishop of Canterbury at Grantham House in 1779-80; and the famous actress, Sarah Siddons at Bristol House in 1795 (which she described as a 'little nutshell upon Putney Heath').[9]

76. Edward Gibbon, 1737-94, author of The Decline and Fall of the Roman Empire, *who was born at Lime Grove, Putney, and spent part of his childhood at the house east of St Mary's Church.*

75. Lime Grove in 1843. It stood close to the eastern corner of Putney Hill and the Upper Richmond Road, and was demolished in about 1862. Its grounds extended as far as East Putney Station and the top of Putney Hill.

Only two other parts of the parish seem to have been as desirable as Roehampton: the Lime Grove estate adjoining Putney Hill and the area between Putney Bridge Road and the Thames, where there were two very grand houses – in 1753 occupied by Sir Joshua Vanneck (father of the Sir Joshua who later built Grove House in Roehampton) and Horatio Walpole, brother of the former Prime Minister. Lime Grove was occupied for most of the first half of the century by Edward Gibbon, one of the Directors of the South Sea Company. His son, also Edward Gibbon, author of *The Decline and Fall of the Roman Empire*, was born there in 1737. Later occupants included Robert Wood, author of *The Ruins of Palmyra* (1753), which was important in spreading knowledge of classical architecture, in 1771, and the Duke of Norfolk in 1772-4.[10]

The villas were generally used as summer houses. Most of their owners had a house in London, and sometimes a stately home (or several stately homes) elsewhere in the country. As already indicated, they were intended to be of modest size. Mount Clare, for example, had only a hall, dining room, saloon and small study on its main floor, with service accommodation in the basement and bedrooms on the upper floor. In these respects the villas were similar to their seventeenth-century predecessors in Putney. Where the villas differed was in the occupants' attitude to the local community and to their surroundings. In the seventeenth century the occupants of the great houses had played a full part in local life, sitting on the parish Vestry and filling local offices such as churchwarden. By the second half of the eighteenth century such duties were left to tradesmen and lesser gentry.[11] Many of the villa occupants attended the exclusive Roehampton Chapel rather than the large and overcrowded Putney Church. Also, whereas people had formerly been happy to build their mansions next to the street, the villa occupants expected much more seclusion and at least a few acres of grounds. Frances Chambers of Ashbourne House in Putney High Street wrote in 1822 of 'the very great molestation it is to have small houses immediately overlooking my garden and field on the Richmond Road corner', and a Mr Johnson wrote in 1786 that his 'very pretty villa' (Bristol House) 'unfortunately stands so immediately upon the Common that it is as much expos'd to the inspection and intrusion of passengers as a street house in London'; this, he claimed, made it necessary to enclose three acres of common beside it (now the

77. The Todd family, the last occupants of Fairfax House, in its garden in 1868.

northern part of Heathview Gardens).[12] Great efforts were made to achieve the necessary seclusion and space: building high brick walls, buying adjacent land, particularly to provide gardens for the houses in Putney High Street, and even shifting main roads. This happened to Putney Hill outside Lime Grove and North House and to Roehampton Lane outside Downshire House and the Cedars.[13] Judging by their occupants, the houses in Putney High Street were now less prestigious than those elsewhere.

We know far too little about how the occupants of the new villas amused themselves. Lady Bessborough wrote in 1798 that 'We are still at Roehampton, and leading much the same life - that is reading, drawing, riding, a little musick, and a great deal of piquet'; her husband was shooting every day at Wimbledon.[14] Great pride was clearly taken in gardens, and heavy expenditure was lavished on them. An estate plan of Downshire House in 1798, for example, shows greenhouse, hothouse, succession house, peach-house, melon ground, Dutch flower garden, two kitchen gardens and the obligatory lawns, shrubbery walks and garden temple.[15] At Manresa House there were a gardener and 12 labourers at work in 1793, and in 1841 gardening was the single most common occupation at Roehampton.[16] The gardens of the villas and great houses occupied nearly 10% of all the unbuilt-on land in the parish in 1783.[17]

DECLINE AND FALL

By the second half of the nineteenth century the large houses in the lower part of Putney were threatened by building development, and the site of one house, Putney Palace, had already been built over. The two houses between Putney Bridge Road and the Thames disappeared in 1853 and Lime Grove in the early 1860s, followed by all the major High Street houses and Putney House in the Upper Richmond Road between 1868 and 1887. One of the last was Fairfax House, the most picturesque house in the High Street, and a campaign was waged in 1887 to save it. Not everyone was sympathetic: the *Observer* considered that 'if every house no more important than that now threatened at Putney was to be left standing, England would get littered with tumble-down buildings dangerous to the lieges and of no interest except to little knots of antiquaries'. The house was found to be unsuitable for public use, so it was decided to turn it into a gentlemen's club and 'residential chambers'. Unfortunately it proved impossible to reach agreement with the owner, Mr Pettiward, on the price, and the campaign had to be abandoned; Montserrat Road now crosses the site.[18] The only survivor in the lower part of Putney is Winchester House, now the Constitutional Club. This is believed to date from about 1730 and its west wing from about 1760.[19]

In the upper part of Putney and at Roehampton the large houses were threatened, somewhat less severely, by declining demand for large houses there. Roehampton became much less exclusive from 1846 once there was a railway so close as Barnes Common. Some houses passed into institutional use, starting with the Convent of the Sacred Heart at Elm Grove in 1850. The Jesuits acquired Manresa House from the Earl of Bessborough in 1861, and the Priory became a nursing home in 1871. During the First World War, Roehampton House and Gifford House became hospitals, and the former has retained that role to the present. In 1921 Grove House was acquired by the Froebel Institute.

78. A reminder of the hundreds of domestic servants in the great houses of Putney and Roehampton: the porch of Fairfax House, c.1880.

79. The Cokayne family in the garden of Ashbourne House, Putney High Street, in about 1868. Norroy Road now runs through the site.

80. *Ashburton House, as rebuilt in the 1850s; demolished in about 1950.*

81. *The Melville family in the grounds of Roehampton House in 1870. The house was occupied by the Earls of Leven and Melville from about 1860 to 1910. It became a hospital (now known as Queen Mary's University Hospital) in 1915.*

82. *The drawing room at Gifford House, c.1910.*

Those houses which remained in private ownership seem to have undergone a change of function, becoming more like country houses than villas. Mount Clare, for example, acquired large Victorian additions, which have since been removed again. This may have been because, for the first time, some of the houses were the sole residence of their occupants. For example, Lady Charlotte Schreiber rented Exeter House as her only residence from 1857 to 1863, throwing parties there once a week and making frequent visits to London theatres (reached by train or by driving, which took three-quarters of an hour).[20] Roehampton still attracted the very rich, such as the American financier, John Pierpoint Morgan, who occupied Dover House until his death in 1913, but no longer the nobility. After the 1870s the only titled occupant was the Earl of Leven and Melville. A few houses were rebuilt - in the case of Gifford House on a spectacular scale.

The first demolitions were of Bristol House in about 1898 and the Cedars in about 1912. Dover House was demolished in 1921 and many others in the 1930s, including Clarence Lodge, Lower Grove House, Bowling Green House, Wildcroft, Highlands, Granard Lodge, Exeter House, Grantham House and North House.[21] The one survivor on Putney Hill, Lower Park, dating from about 1800, was converted into flats. Elm Grove was damaged in the Second World War and later demolished. By 1949 none of the great houses were in private ownership. The remaining ones along Putney Heath made way for the Ashburton Estate in about 1950. Those whose grounds were taken for the Alton Estate have survived in institutional use - for example Downshire House as part of the University of Greenwich.

83. Gifford House, as rebuilt in about 1894; demolished in about 1950.

A Modern Babylon

According to the *Wandsworth Borough News* in 1887, if Fairfax House were to be demolished (as shortly afterwards happened), 'then Putney loses its individuality and sinks into the position of a prosperous but a prosaic modern suburb of the nineteenth-century Babylon'.[1] In fact that process was already well advanced by 1887.

The arrival of the railway at Putney in 1846 had little immediate impact, but the pace of building was certainly quickening. The developments of the mid-nineteenth century now form some of Putney's most prized Conservation Areas. By 1849 small villas had appeared in 'the Gardens', comprising Charlwood Road, Hotham Villas and part of Clarendon Drive, and some of these survive. The cottages in Parkfields and the west side of Coalecroft Road (originally Lower and Upper Parkfields) were built between about 1846 and 1860 by Henry Scarth, a local solicitor. Stratford Grove was under construction at the time of the 1851 census: the land was owned by William Stratford, and the building was probably undertaken by his son John, a builder who lived in Roehampton High Street and employed five men. In 1851 the first four houses were occupied, one was finished but vacant and ten more were under construction.[2]

A more prestigious development was the Cedars, by the river north of Deodar Road, in 1853. As built, it consisted of two terraces each of 17 five-storey houses, with a communal garden between the houses and the river, but the original plan included terraces around three sides of a garden between the present Florian and Merivale Roads. With a few variations, each house consisted of kitchen and offices in the basement; hall, dining room and library or morning room on the ground floor; two drawing rooms and conservatory on the first floor; and seven bedrooms, a dressing room and a bathroom on the upper three floors. Construction of the District Railway in 1889 caused the demolition of three of the houses and probably made the remainder hard to let, and the terraces were demolished soon afterwards.[3]

The first really large area to be developed was the Lime Grove Estate, occupying the whole of the area east of Putney Hill, in the mid-1860s, inaugurating the main period of suburban development. In this period the developer-builders like the Stratfords became

84. A recently discovered photograph, taken from south of the railway cutting in about 1869, just at the start of the transformation of Putney High Street. Beyond the railway, where Putney's first station can be seen, are wooden scaffolding poles for the High Street's first parade of Victorian shops (between Disraeli Road and Putney Station). On the far side of the High Street is Ashbourne House, which survived until 1887.

85. Putney High Street in 1865.

86. The Cedars, built in 1853 and demolished c.1890.

87. Advertisement for new houses in Colinette Road (laid out in 1878) and Upper Richmond Road.

Colinett Road, PUTNEY, S.W. | Upper Richmond Rd. PUTNEY, S.W.

ACCOMMODATION.

Second Floor —
Five Bedrooms.
Linen Press (over H. W. Tank).
Housemaid's Sink and W.C.
Staircase to Box Room in Roof.

First Floor (Ceiling 10 ft.)—
Three Spacious Bedrooms.
Bath Room.
Dressing Room.
W.C.

Ground Floor (Ceiling 11 ft.)—
Drawing Room.
Dining Room and Alcove.
Library.
Cloak Room and Lavatory with Hot & Cold Supplies.
W.C.
Hall, Vestibule, and Porch.
Side Entrance to Garden.

Basement (Ceiling 8 ft. 6 in.)—
Kitchen, Butler's Pantry.
Housekeeper's Room.
Two Larders, 2 Store Rooms.
Wine, Beer and Coal Cellars.
Trades' Entrance, Servants' W.C.

ACCOMMODATION.

Second Floor (Ceiling 9 ft. 6 in.)—
Four Bedrooms (1 adapted for Billiard Room).
Linen Press (over H. W. Tank).
Housemaid's Sink, W.C., &c.
Staircase to Box Room in Roof.

First Floor (Ceiling 10 ft. 6 in.)—
Four Spacious Bedrooms.
Dressing Room.
Bath Room, W.C.

Ground Floor (Ceiling 12 ft.)—
Drawing Room, leading to Con[illegible] 15 ft. by 10 ft. 9 in.
Dining Room.
Library.
Cloak Room, W.C., and Lavatory with Hot and Cold Supplies.
Entrance to Garden at back.
Tesselated Hall, Vestibule, and Porch.

Basement (Ceiling 9 ft.)—
Kitchen, Butler's Pantry, fitted
Housekeeper's Room.
Two Larders, Boot Room.
Store Rooms, Wine, Beer, and Coal Cellars.
Potting Shed under Conservatory, with Entrance to Garden.
Trades' Entrance, Servants' W.C.

The Houses on this Estate are built in a most substantial manner, are thoroughly dry, and fit for immediate Occupation. Gravel Subsoil. The Officer of the Sanitary Protection Association has recently reported that "The Drainage System is based upon the most modern ideas of Sanitary Science, and in perfect working order."

The Situation is one of the best in this Charming Locality, within a few minutes walk of Wimbledon and Barnes Commons, and Richmond Park; and the Railway communication to all parts is very good.

For further particulars apply to—

D. SWANSON,
8, COLINETT ROAD, PUTNEY, S.W.

88. Builders of Victorian Putney: Mr H. Roffey and his workmen outside the almost-completed Putney Library in Disraeli Road, c.1898.

rarer. Instead, in most cases, the landowner or developer laid out the street and the drains, and blocks of building sites were then sold on 99-year leases. The blocks tended to become larger over time, as indicated by comparing the mixture of styles in the relatively early Disraeli Road with the greater uniformity of later streets such as Norroy Road. The builders were usually local firms, such as Adamson's, whose yard is now occupied by Sainsbury's supermarket, and W.H. Pearce of Felsham Road, who built Redgrave Road and Festing Road. Usually they built houses – detached, semi-detached or terraced – but there were some blocks of flats, notably Kenilworth Court of 1901-3.

The two large developments of the 1850s and 1860s – the Cedars and Lime Grove – were both of very substantial houses, but Disraeli Road, laid out in 1866, was more significant for the future – the first long street of smaller houses for the lower middle class. Thereafter, building proceeded at a furious pace: there were 15 new streets in the 1860s, ten in the 1870s, 27 in the 1880s, 16 in the 1890s and 13 in the 1900s (see table), although the laying out of a street was often just the beginning of a lengthy building process. Building materials flooded in: in 1881 Robert Avis's yard at Baltic Wharf, Brewhouse Lane, was receiving bricks from Nuneaton, Huntingdon and Kent, stone from Yorkshire and the Bath area, and timber from Godalming; presumably there was also slate from north Wales.[4] The parish's population rose from 3,811 in 1831 to 6,481 in 1861, 17,777 in 1891 and 28,242 in 1911.

The key decade was the 1880s, which saw the creation of an astonishing amount of present-day Putney. As well as the 27 new streets and many new shops, there was a new bridge, opened in 1886, a new station on the existing railway (1886), a new railway serving East Putney complete with a new Thames bridge (1889), and the Embankment, constructed in 1887-8. The latter was a source of particular pride to the growing town. On 27 March 1888, with flags and bunting displayed and the bells of St Mary's ringing, a crowd of a thousand people walked the full length of the Embankment and back to declare it open.[5] The 1880s was also when much of old Putney disappeared, including the last of the great houses in the High Street, which became a purely business street. In fact few London suburbs have retained so little of

89. *Architect's drawing of Richmond Mansions (now University Mansions) in the Lower Richmond Road, April 1900.*

their pre-Victorian past, probably reflecting the fact that Putney's older buildings were almost all in the main streets, where there was least chance of them surviving.

The last two substantial developments before the First World War were Landford and Earldom Roads in 1906 and the much larger Westbury Estate, centred on Hazlewell Road, from 1903. These seem to have kept the builders busy until the First World War halted further activity. By the outbreak of war, Putney north of the Upper Richmond Road and east of the Hill was almost fully built up, but to the south-west the houses of Woodborough Road, Luttrell Avenue and Chartfield Avenue formed the edge of the continuously built-up area, beyond which there had been little change. Westleigh Avenue had been laid out in 1912, but by the end of the war was grass-grown, with few houses, and a field bounded by Westleigh, Chartfield and Genoa Avenues was used to graze the occasional flock of sheep, later to be driven through the streets to a butcher in the High Street.

VICTORIAN INHABITANTS

Victorian Putney was largely middle class, with relatively few poor families. When Charles Booth compiled his map of poverty in London in 1898-9, dividing residential streets into seven social categories, the two poorest categories were not represented in Putney at all. Late nineteenth-century Putney seems to have become a by-word for prosperous and contented but unremarkable existence, except to moralists such as the Presbyterian Minister in 1902, who criticised its 'atmosphere of pleasure-seeking' and its 'low moral level...though mainly a middle-class district'.[6] In Anthony Trollope's *Small House at Allington* (1864), Mr Butterwell, a civil servant, 'lived a pleasant, easy, smiling life in a villa at Putney', and hoped 'that he might achieve some sort of Putney villa in the world beyond'. In Arnold Bennett's *Buried Alive* (1908), which is largely set in Putney,

'Putney was a place where you lived unvexed, untroubled. You had your little house, and your furniture, and your ability to look after yourself at all ends, and your knowledge of the prices of everything... You were never worried by ambitions, or by envy, or by the desire to know

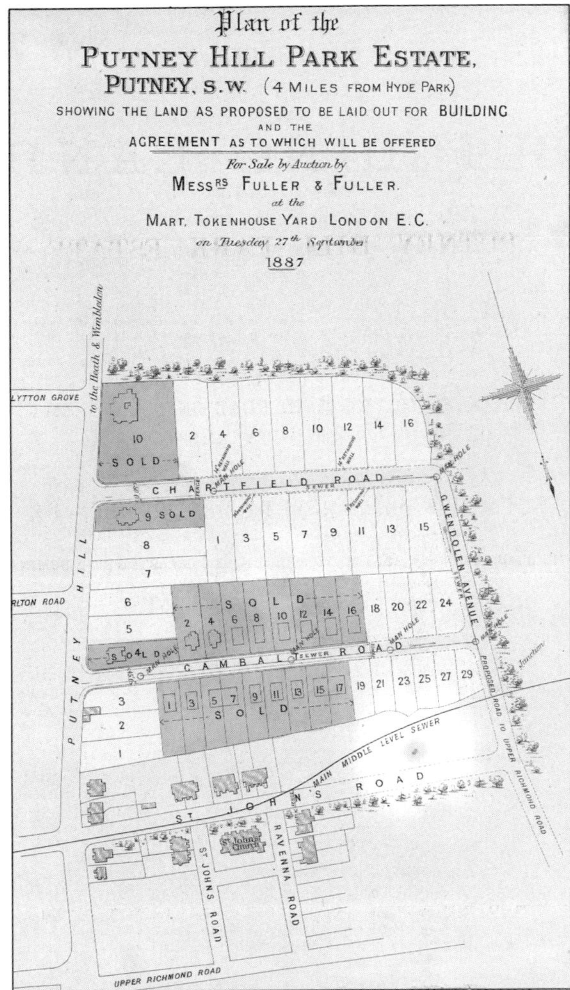

90. *The grounds of Lower Park, as laid out for building in 1887, with a few houses already built. The eastern ends of Chartfield Avenue, Cambalt Road and St John's Avenue are all shown as blocked off by fences. Lower Park (top left-hand corner of the shaded area) has outlasted almost all the houses built in its grounds.*

precisely what the wealthy did and to do likewise...You were rich, for the reason that you spent less than you received. You never speculated about the ultimate cause of things, or puzzled yourself concerning the possible developments of society in the next hundred years... Existence at Putney... seemed to breathe of romance – the romance of common sense and kindliness and simplicity.'

The 1891 census (the most recent available) reveals a very different Putney from that of 1851. The daily commuter had arrived in force, and Putney was now even more thoroughly populated with City men, tradesmen and professional people of all kinds, with a much greater variety of occupations. There was also

91. *Cambalt Road, looking west, c.1905.*

a very large number of householders described as 'living on their own means' (presumably investments, annuities and pensions). According to Booth in 1902, 'the rich and the middle class are either "retired" or employed in the City: they go into business by the District or London and South Western Railway services. There are also a large number of theatrical people attracted by the late trains on both lines'. Booth thought that the wealthy were tending to leave, either for 'regions of fashion' in west London or out of the metropolis altogether, being replaced by 'a well-to-do class forming a semi-genteel aristocracy'. He added that 'Newness is a feature of middle class Putney. The rich and the poor are those who have been there longest'.[7]

We can explore late Victorian Putney with the help of the 1891 census, sale catalogues and Booth's map of 1898-9. The map demonstrates the association often found in London between height above sea level and affluence. His richest class, the wealthy, were to be found by the Heath, on the Lime Grove Estate, and in Cambalt Road, Chartfield Avenue, part of St John's Avenue west of the Hill, and the north side of the Upper Richmond Road west of Quill Bridge. An example is 'Elmhurst', 23 Carlton Drive, approached from the road by a carriage drive and containing offices and billiard room in the basement, dining room, drawing room (33 by 17 feet) and conservatory on the ground floor, and 11 bedrooms, a dressing room and a bathroom on the top two floors.[8] Typical inhabitants on the Lime Grove Estate were barristers and solicitors, City men such as stockbrokers, merchants, company secretaries and directors, and surveyors, civil engineers and other professional people. The fifteen householders in Cambalt Road in 1891 comprised five living on their own means, three lawyers, two members of the Stock Exchange, one architect and retired builder, one watch manufacturer, one mechanical engineer and diamond merchant, one marine underwriter and insurance broker, and the secretary of the Ottoman Railway Company. These houses typically had three servants in 1891 – most often cook, housemaid and parlourmaid or

92. *Werter Road, c.1906.*

93. *Putney Hill, c.1907.*

nurse. Streets such as Carlton Drive and Cambalt Road can be regarded as whole streets of villas, with smaller gardens and fewer servants than the eighteenth-century villas but little different in size and having the same effects on the local economy. Relatively few of the houses in this category survive, but they include Rosslyn Tower in St John's Avenue (1873) and the 'Nelson houses' (*c*.1865) on the north side of the Upper Richmond Road west of Quill Bridge (named after the sister of the third Earl Nelson, who married the heir to the Pettiward estate in 1855).

Booth's second class, the 'well-to-do' was much more numerous. An example from Werter Road is Preston Lodge, which in 1885 had drawing room, dining room, kitchen and offices, breakfast room, three bedrooms, bathroom, two attics, cellars, and a 'large garden and croquet lawn'. The occupants of Werter Road in 1891 included clerks, commercial travellers and agents, tradesmen, stockjobbers and teachers. The houses may have been too large for their location, as a quarter of them had been subdivided and six householders were described as lodging-house keepers. Most houses had one or two servants, typically cook and housemaid.

The next class, the 'fairly comfortable', reckoned by Booth to be higher class labour in supervisory positions, was also numerous. In addition there were many streets which fell between 'fairly comfortable' and 'well-to-do', including Norroy, Chelverton and Disraeli Roads, and the majority of the houses in these had servants (usually only one), but the 'fairly comfortable' roads had hardly any domestic servants. An example is Weiss Road, with 36 houses, each divided into two dwellings of three rooms. Here the 69 householders in 1891 included 20 involved in transport or horsekeeping, 11 in the building trades, six craftsmen such as printers and a wheelwright, seven foremen, clerks or assistants, four policemen, three postmen and four labourers. None had servants.

Booth's next two categories (the poorest recorded in Putney) included only a few streets, many of them dating from before the 1860s. 'Poverty and comfort (mixed)' takes in Lifford Street, Charlwood Terrace, Walkers Place, parts of the eastern end of Felsham Road, the Platt, the western part of Weimar Street and March's Place (behind the Half Moon). Only the first two of these survive. Lifford Street, for example, had 38 houses of five or six rooms in 1891, of which 24 were subdivided. The mixture of occupations was similar to that in Weiss Road, but with a smattering of charwomen, laundresses and manglers.

'Moderate poverty' applied to Olivette Street, Mascotte Road, Brewhouse Lane, part of the Quill/Lacy Road triangle, Gay Street, River Street and Biggs Row and neighbouring alleys. Booth noted the existence of 'old village poverty connected with labourers in market gardens and riverside work'. In the streets around the Platt he was told that 'Some of the men live on the prostitution of their wives, or on their labour as laundresses. Others are connected with the river as boatmen and boat attendants, and the rest are, or call themselves, labourers'.[9] In the 1891 census the inhabitants of the poorer streets were typically labourers, watermen, painters, carmen, cab drivers, horsekeepers, laundresses or charwomen. In Olivette Street in 1891, with three rooms per house, the most common occupations were horsekeeper, labourer and printer. Some of the poorest housing was to be found in the alleys off the High Street, such as Wilkins Court, entered through an archway to the right of the Spotted Horse, but these were too small to show up on Booth's map. Almost all the areas of moderate poverty have been cleared, usually for council housing, but Olivette Street and Mascotte Road survive.

NEW STREETS IN PUTNEY 1864-1912

CLASS *(1898/9)*	NAME	DATE
	East of Putney Hill	
1	Lytton Grove	1866
1	Mercier Rd	1867
1	Carlton Drive	1867
1	Rayner's Rd	1867
1	St John's Ave	1867
1	Kersfield Rd	1868
	East of High St	
2/3	Disraeli Rd	1866/9
2	Werter Rd	1875/6
	Rockland Rd	1878
3	Winthorpe Rd	1878
2	Atney Rd	1880
2	Burstock Rd	1880
2	Montserrat Rd (E)	1880
2	Montserrat Rd (W)	1887
2/3	Florian Rd	1892
3	Merivale Rd	1892
	North of Lower Richmond Rd	
	Pentlow St	1866
	Sefton St	1866
2	Ruvigny Gdns	1880
	Floss St	1884
	Ashlone Rd	1887
3	Festing Rd	1887
3	Rotherwood Rd	1891
3	Bendemeer Rd	1893
3	Gladwyn Rd	1893
3	Glendarvon St	1895
	Danemere St	1898

	North of Felsham Rd	
3	Bemish Rd	1867
2/3	Stanbridge Rd	1868/77
2/3	Fanthorpe St	1877
3	Wymond St	1877
3	Weiss Rd	1886
2/3	Roskell Rd	1887
3	Salvin Rd	1887
2/3	Farlow Rd	1892
	North of Hotham Rd	
2/3	Felsham Rd (W)	1877
3	Gwalior Rd	1881
5	Mascotte Rd	1882
5	Olivette St	1882
3	Redgrave Rd	1892
	Abbotstone Rd	1893
	Bangalore St	1898
3	Blackett St	1898
	Borneo St	1898
	Westhorpe Rd	1898
	West of High St	
4	Lifford St	1866
3 & 2/3	Erpingham Rd	1877/84
2	Dryburgh Rd	1884
2	Egliston Rd	1884
2/3	Norroy Rd	1886
2/3	Chelverton Rd	1887
	Clarendon Drive (W)	1891
	Hotham Rd (W)	1898/1906
	Rossdale Rd	1899
	Earldom Rd	1906
	Landford Rd	1906
	Gamlen Rd	1912
	West of Putney Hill	
2	Burston Rd	1864
2	Ravenna Rd	1864
1 & 2	St John's Ave	1867
2	Ulva Rd	1870
2	Colinette Rd	1878
2	Dealtry Rd	1878
1	Cambalt Rd	1883
1	Chartfield Ave (E)	1883
2	Gwendolen Ave (N)	1883
2	Carmalt Gdns	1886
2	Balmuir Gdns	1889
	Bramcote Rd	1889
	Briar Walk	1889
	Gwendolen Ave (S)	1889/92
	Howards Lane (E)	1889/1903
	Woodborough Rd	1889
	Woodthorpe Rd	1889
	Campion Rd	1903
	Enmore Rd	1903
	Hazlewell Rd	1903
	Holroyd Rd	1903
	Larpent Ave	1903/6
	Luttrell Ave	1903/6
	Tideswell Rd	1903
	Montolieu Gdns	1904
	Castello Ave	1905
	Chartfield Ave (W)	1905/6
	Genoa Ave	1905/12
	St Simon's Ave	1905
	Westleigh Ave	1912

Note: The dates are when the street was first named or house numbers were assigned to a new section of an existing street, not necessarily when the houses were built. Present-day street names are given where they differ from the original. Booth's map does not cover the area west of Colinette Road.

Key to classes: 1 - wealthy; 2 - well-to-do; 3 - fairly comfortable; 4 - poverty and comfort (mixed); 5 - moderate poverty.

Source: London County Council, *Names of streets and places in the administrative County of London* (4th edn., 1955); Booth, vol. 5.

SOME VICTORIAN RESIDENTS

The author and dramatist, Douglas Jerrold, contributor to *Punch* and author of *Mrs Caudle's Curtain Lectures,* lived at West Lodge (on the site of Putney

94. *Douglas Jerrold.*

95. Jenny Lind.

96. Theodore Watts Dunton and the poet Charles Swinburne (seated) in the garden of the Pines, Putney Hill.

Hospital) from 1845 to about 1854. The great literary figures of the day visited him there, often finding themselves required to join in games. After one dinner party, 'the hearty host, with his guests, including Mr Charles Dickens, Mr Maclise, Mr Macready, and Mr John Forster, indulged in a most active game of leap-frog...Never were boys more completely possessed by the spirit of the game... and foremost among the players and laughers was the little figure of Douglas Jerrold, his hair flowing wildly, and his face radiant with pleasure'.[10]

Jenny Lind (1820-87), the most famous singer of her day (known as 'the Swedish Nightingale'), came to England in 1847. In 1855 she and her husband rented Laurel House in Putney High Street (mid-way between Disraeli and Werter Roads), where their son could have 'good air', and in 1858 they moved to Roehampton Lodge (on the site of Daylesford Avenue), moving again to Parkside in the following year.[11]

Putney's most famous Victorian resident was the poet, Charles Swinburne, invited by his friend Theodore Watts Dunton to Putney to save him from his damaging lifestyle. Swinburne lived with Watts Dunton at the Pines, Putney Hill (which still stands) from 1879 until his death in 1909. He was to be seen most days walking briskly across the Common to Wimbledon.

Another resident was Lawrence Oates, son of a gentleman and explorer, born in Putney in 1880. He spent much of his childhood at what is now 309 Upper Richmond Road.[12] In 1910 he set out with Scott's Antarctic Expedition, and was one of the five to reach the South Pole in January 1912. On the return journey, Oates, crippled by frostbite, decided that his presence could fatally delay his companions, and sacrificed his life by walking out into the blizzard, saying 'I'm just going outside and I may be some time'.

THE DEVELOPMENT OF URBAN LIFE

Putney gradually took on the characteristics of a substantial town in the late nineteenth century, with new shops, schools, churches and leisure facilities, mostly described in later chapters. However, it never acquired its own town hall. For centuries it had been linked with Mortlake and Wimbledon as part of the same manor, but this ceased to have much significance in the seventeenth century, when the main body of local administration was the parish Vestry. When the Poor Law Reform Act of 1834 created a system of large Poor Law Unions covering a number of parishes, Putney Parish became part of Wandsworth Union, and this seems to have set the pattern for the future. Upon the creation of the Metropolitan

97. Putney Market, an arcade of shops between Putney High Street and Brewhouse Lane, c.1908. It was not very successful, and lasted only from about 1908 to the early 1920s. Demolished in 1937.

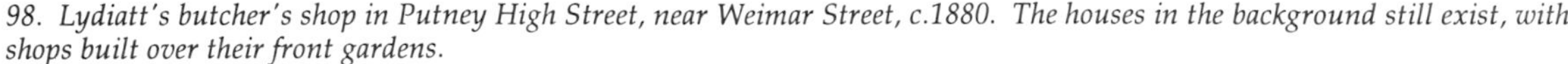

98. Lydiatt's butcher's shop in Putney High Street, near Weimar Street, c.1880. The houses in the background still exist, with shops built over their front gardens.

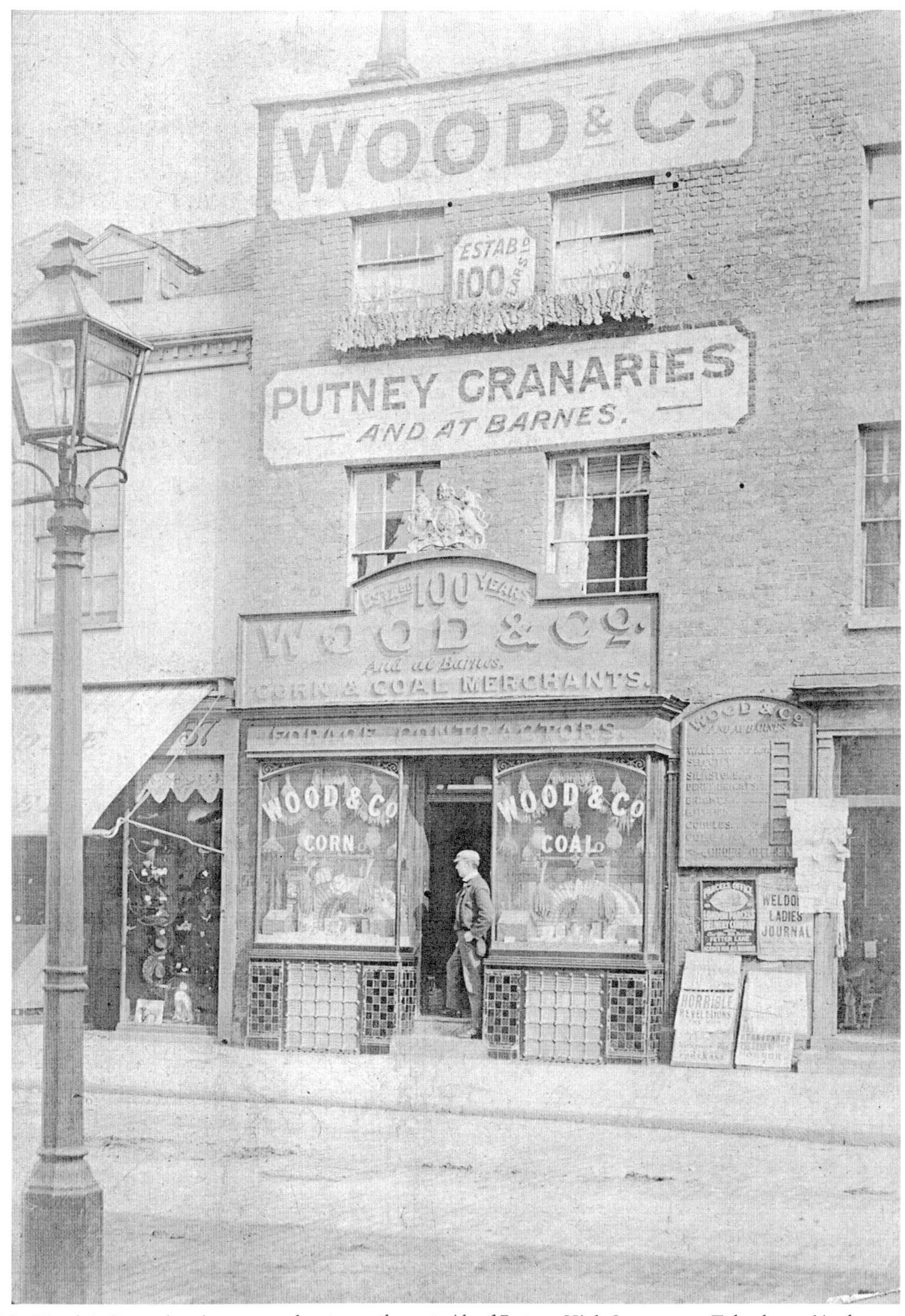

99. *Wood & Co, coal and corn merchants, on the east side of Putney High Street, near Tokenhouse Yard, c.1890. One of the newspaper placards promises 'horrible revelations'.*

100. Mrs Slater's 'general shop', facing the Lower Common opposite the Putney Hospital site, c.1905. Miss Ellen Slater is standing in the doorway.

101. Cake made by E. Schur of 24 Putney High Street, c.1913, 16 feet high and weighing 7 tons, to commemorate. the '21st Annual International Exhibition and Market'.

Board of Works in 1855, Putney Parish became part of its Wandsworth District. Once it had become attached to Wandsworth in this way, it naturally became part of the London County Council upon its creation in 1888 (being on the outer edge of the LCC's area) and of Wandsworth Borough Council in 1899. It did not become a separate parliamentary constituency until 1918.

The Metropolitan Police District was extended to Putney in 1830. By 1851 there was a police station at No 1 Priests Bridge, on the very edge of the parish, and ten policemen lived in the parish. The present site in the Upper Richmond Road came into use in about 1870.[13]

Putney obtained gas lighting in 1834, a piped water supply in 1857-8 and electric lighting in 1896. The reservoir on the Heath was not for Putney's benefit: the water, pumped up from the Thames at Thames Ditton, was taken across the river towards Chelsea and Westminster, at first by means of an aqueduct and later by pipes under the footways of the present bridge.[14]

Putney's local newspaper was founded in 1884 by a Mr Patching of Putney High Street as the *Putney and South Western Chronicle*. Within a year it had become the *Putney and Wandsworth Borough News*, the words *Putney and* later being dropped. In 1885 it was bought

102. *Morrison's dairy in the Lower Richmond Road, c.1910.*

103. *Shops on the west side of Putney High Street between Lacy Road and Felsham Road, c.1907.*

104. Putney Police Station in 1908. It was replaced by the present building in 1934-5.

by Putney's first MP, Henry Kimber, who retained control until 1923 and used the paper to promote Conservatism.[15]

Putney Library was established in 1888. The present building and site, which came into use eleven years later, were donated by Sir George Newnes, a self-made man who began his career as a clerk and then made enough money running a vegetarian restaurant in Manchester to establish a mass-circulation magazine (*Tit-Bits*), which made his fortune. He lived at Wildcroft on Putney Heath.[16]

Putney had no hospitals until the twentieth century. Putney Hospital resulted from a bequest of £75,000 by Sir Henry Chester (d.1900), together with further fund-raising and the donation of a site by Sir William Lancaster. At its opening in 1912 it had only 25 beds, but it was subsequently enlarged. Queen Mary's University Hospital came into existence in 1915, as a hospital for limbless war casualties, and pioneered the treatment of amputees. It remained part of the War Pensioners' Group of Hospitals until it joined the National Health Service in 1961. The Eileen Lecky Health Centre in Clarendon Drive also deserves to be mentioned; it originated in 1914 in

105. Caricature of Sir George Newnes, 1851-1910, who donated the present Putney Library in Disraeli Road.

106. Pumping out water at the lower end of Putney High Street after a flood in 1909.

Felsham Road as the Children's Health Centre, and following fund-raising in 1931, Eileen Lecky and Ann Gibbs were able to build and run the present centre. The Centre subsequently passed to Wandsworth Borough Council.

The new inhabitants of Victorian Putney eventually had to be buried. Both St Mary's churchyard and the Old Burial Ground in the Upper Richmond Road were closed under the Burials Act 1853, and a new burial ground was obtained on the Lower Common in 1855, following which many a sad little procession wended its way across the Lower Common. A nearby resident referred to 'the pathetic sound of the tolling bell on Saturday afternoons, mingling so curiously with the cheerful voices of the children and the cricketers'. When this cemetery proved too small, part of Newlands Farm in Putney Vale was bought, and the first burial in Putney Vale Cemetery took place in 1891.[17]

107. Architect's drawing of Putney Hospital, as built. The hospital opened in 1912, and is now greatly altered.

108. The reading room of Putney Library in 1900.

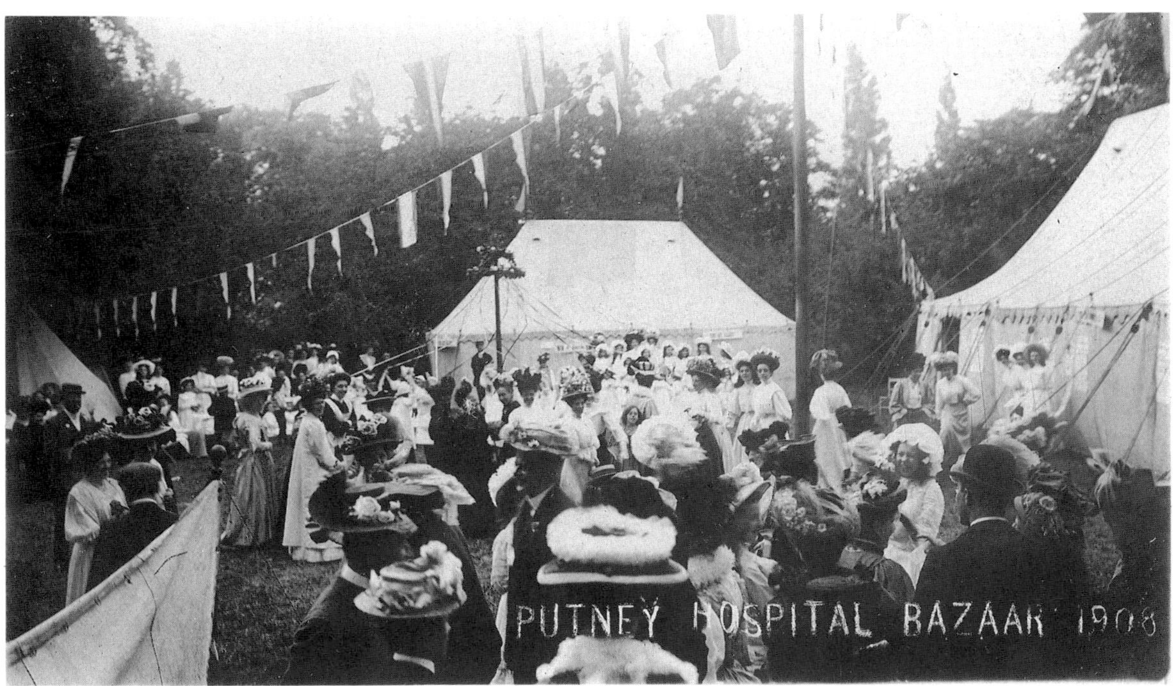

109. Fund-raising bazaar for Putney Hospital in 1908.

110. Coronation Day in Putney High Street, 1902.

VICTORIAN AND EDWARDIAN ROEHAMPTON

Victorian and Edwardian Roehampton grew significantly, but not as rapidly as Putney: from about 950 inhabitants in 1851 to 2,584 in 1911. Most of present-day Roehampton village dates from the mid-Victorian period, including Ponsonby Road, laid out in 1863, and Stamford Cottages and Elizabeth Place on opposite sides of Medfield Street and dated 1862 and 1870 respectively. The village also acquired a school (1836 and 1854), a Catholic church (1881) and an Anglican church (1896-8). The one large mid-Victorian development outside the village itself was the Roehampton Park Estate (chiefly Alton and Bessborough Roads), laid out in the 1860s in the grounds of Manresa House - contemporary with the Lime Grove Estate and with houses of similar opulence. The next major developments were not until the late 1890s: Rodway Road and the roads off it in 1897, Heathview Gardens in 1898, and Daylesford, Langside and Dungarvan Avenues in 1906.[18]

Roehampton remained small and relatively remote: in 1902 Charles Booth wrote that it 'seems to lie a long way from anywhere, except to such as have private carriages... and the impression of remoteness is intensified when we read that on the royal birthday teachers and school children sang the National Anthem "on the green"'.[19]

112. Roehampton village seen from the east in 1841. The building on the left is the classroom and teacher's house of the school (now Roehampton Church School), built in 1836.

113. Roehampton High Street, c.1903.

111. Roehampton High Street, c.1900.

On the Move

Steam-powered transport first appeared in Putney in the form of boats rather than trains. The London and Westminster Steamboat Company began to serve Putney in 1838, much to the distress of the inhabitants of the Lower Richmond Road, who found smoke and soot coming in their windows.[1] In 1882 competition from river services was credited with keeping down railway fares from Putney to Waterloo. However, steamboat services on the Thames ceased in 1909.[2] Attempts to establish regular services on the river have occurred from time to time ever since, but without lasting success.

RAILWAYS

A railway was first proposed through Putney in 1836, and would have crossed the High Street further north than the present line (about on the line of Montserrat Road), but this was not proceeded with.[3] The existing line was proposed by the Richmond Railway Company in 1845, with the backing of the London & South Western Railway (LSWR). It was to connect Richmond with the LSWR's main line at Falcon Lane (now Clapham Junction). Putney Vestry, which perhaps feared an influx of working class residents, opposed it as 'not only inexpedient but totally unnecessary', arguing that the parish already had 'all reasonable and expeditious means afforded them at a trifling expense of going to and from London and Richmond'.[4] Nevertheless the line received parliamentary approval and opened in July 1846. Trains at first ran to the LSWR terminus at Nine Elms, but from 1848 to Waterloo. The train service in 1851 was roughly hourly and the journey to Waterloo took only about 20 minutes, little slower than today, and less than half the time taken by the stage coaches and omnibuses. No freight service was provided: goods had to be collected by cart from Barnes Station or brought by river. The type of traffic catered for at first is indicated by the timetable and fares. The first up train left Putney at 8.06 am, reaching Waterloo at 8.30. The fares ranged from 9d single in first class to 5½d in third class, and only four trains a day offered third class accommodation.[5] The pattern of Victorian working hours would have made these trains useless to artisans or wage-earning clerks in the City, and they were also too expensive; the working classes had neither time nor money for long daily journeys. Instead the railway catered for the professional and business classes such as Putney's numerous lawyers and bankers.

114. Putney Station in 1846, the year it opened.

115. Barges at the drawdock, seen from the present bridge in 1900. In the background on the left the Star and Garter is under construction.

116. East Putney Station, c.1905.

117. Livery stables in the Upper Richmond Road, immediately west of the Fox and Hounds, c.1880.

There was no sudden upsurge in Putney's growth in 1846; after all, numerous other places – some much closer to London – were also acquiring railways at this time. However, railway traffic grew quickly: as early as 1864 the station had to be enlarged, and in 1886 the line was widened to four tracks and most of the present station building erected. By 1887 there were approximately four trains an hour, including nine reaching Waterloo before 9 am. The present station entrance dates from 1902.[6] Trains from Putney Station undoubtedly played a crucial role in the development of Victorian Putney, and the railway may also have had a significant effect on Roehampton, where estate agents' prospectuses began to emphasise the closeness of Barnes Station, just a short carriage ride away.

Putney's second railway resulted less from rational transport planning than from the railway politics of the 1870s and 1880s. The outcome could just as easily have been a line on a different route, with significant consequences for the pattern of development. In 1869 the Metropolitan & District Railway (now the District Line) reached West Brompton, and having spent heavily on its central London track it was anxious to obtain the developing suburban traffic to the south-west. The LSWR was equally determined to defend what it regarded as its territory. In 1872 the District was authorised to extend its line to Richmond via Putney and Barnes: it would have crossed the Thames to reach Putney in the Rotherwood Road area. The LSWR responded by buying off the District with running powers over its own line between Hammersmith and Richmond.[7]

In 1880 the District reached Putney Bridge Station. The following year it was authorised to build a line via the present East Putney Station and across or under Putney Heath to Kingston and Surbiton. A separate, independent scheme, authorised in 1882, was for a line connecting Putney Bridge Station and the LSWR main line at Wimbledon. The latter was strongly backed by J.A. Beaumont, who had bought Wimbledon Park from Earl Spencer and believed the new line would promote its development and double its value. Putney Vestry was again disgruntled, wanting a station in Putney Bridge Road rather than the Upper Richmond Road, and again no notice was taken of it. In the event, both sets of promoters failed to raise enough money, and their powers were passed to the LSWR, which abandoned the Kingston route across Putney Heath but built the Wimbledon line.

118. Roehampton to Putney horse-bus by the fountain at Roehampton, c.1880. In the background is the Montague Arms.

The District was to have running powers to Wimbledon and the LSWR to South Kensington, although the latter were never used.[8]

When the new line opened in 1889, both companies used it for direct services between London and Wimbledon (the LSWR gaining access from the connecting lines east of Putney Station), but the District provided three-quarters of the trains. The railway was at first of limited value to commuters because there were only two trains a day reaching Waterloo and four reaching Mansion House before 9am, but services soon increased. In 1905 the line to Wimbledon was electrified, and by 1914 there were 108 trains a day to Mansion House (more than three times as many as in 1891), including 24 arriving before 9 am. LSWR services from Wimbledon to Waterloo via East Putney were always less frequent, and were not electrified until 1915. They ceased in 1941, since when empty trains returning to the Wimbledon carriage sheds have been the only regular users of the connecting lines.[9] Nevertheless, the whole of the line opened in 1889 remained in the ownership of British Rail until 1994.

Most services through Putney Station were electrified in 1916, but some of the longer-distance ones remained steam-operated until 1939.

ROADS, BUSES AND TRAMS

Railways were fast and relatively comfortable, but omnibuses could provide a greater variety of routes and more of a door-to-door service, as between Roehampton and the Bank. In 1851 there were horse buses at ten-minute intervals from Fulham High Street to the Bank (starting at 7.40 am), and a few which crossed the bridge to reach Roehampton, Wimbledon or Kingston. In 1881 Putney was considered to be one of the London suburbs best served by buses, and the competition they provided to the railway was regarded as a restraint on train fares at Putney.[10] The bus garage in Chelverton Road originated as stables for London General Omnibus Company horses. For local journeys, both omnibuses and hackney cabs were available, and horses and carriages could be hired from livery stables. Only the grandest Victorian developments included facilities for private carriages and horses, such as the mews now known as Earnshaw Place, off Carlton Drive.

In 1880 Putney Bridge was purchased by the Metropolitan Board of Works and freed from tolls, as were Hammersmith and Wandsworth Bridges. One result was that the Fulham horse buses were extended across the bridge and now turned at the White Lion. The old bridge was becoming increasingly unsatisfactory both for road and river traffic, and the Board decided to build a new one. A new site was selected, running directly from the bottom of Putney High Street along the line of the aqueduct built by the

119. Tibbets Corner in about 1907.

Chelsea Waterworks Company in about 1854. The new approaches resulted in the widening of the Lower Richmond Road, which at its eastern end had been little more than the width of a single carriage. The new bridge, of Cornish granite, was designed by Sir Joseph and Mr Edward Bazalgette, well-known for their work on the Thames embankments and London's sewerage and drainage system, and was opened by the Prince of Wales (later Edward VII) in 1886. It was widened in 1931-3, but is otherwise little altered.

Road transport would have difficulty competing with the railways until the slow and costly horse could be dispensed with. Putney acquired its first motor buses in 1901, when F.J. Bell began a service with two single-deckers between Putney and Piccadilly Circus, and its last horse buses disappeared by 1914. Some routes established in the early years of the motor buses continue little changed, such as the 14 and the 37. From 1909, the National Steam Bus Co. operated steam buses, with oil-fired boilers, on several local routes, and these lasted until 1919. According to Osbert Lancaster, Putney Hill's 'immense residential dullness' was 'occasionally relieved by a steam omnibus bursting into flames on approaching the summit'.[11] Electric trams from Hammersmith to Putney began in 1909, terminating outside Kenilworth Court. They were extended along Putney Bridge Road to Wandsworth in 1912, and from 1921 could run through to Clapham Junction, Vauxhall and beyond. From Putney to Hammersmith and to Wandsworth there was a 78-seat tram every three or four minutes.

120. A London Road Car Company motor bus, c.1908. The company had a depot for horse buses and motor buses in Felsham Road opposite Mascotte Road.

The trams were replaced by trolleybuses in 1937, and these by motor buses in 1960.[12] The importance of motor and steam buses and trams was that they provided faster and cheaper journeys than the horse buses could have done, supplementing the increasingly frequent trains but serving a greater range of places.

The story in the rest of the twentieth century has been the immense rise in the number of private cars and lorries and the decline of public transport by road. The result has been increased mobility for some, and more efficient distribution of goods, at the cost of congestion, noise, pollution and accidents. In

121. The Putney Hill trace horse, maintained through charitable contributions in order to help horse-drawn vehicles up the Hill, c.1909.

1908, for example, a prospectus for 25 Chartfield Avenue noted that it was within a quarter of an hour's drive of the West End and had space for 'stabling or a motor house', but also emphasised that the house was sufficiently far from the road to be away from the noise of motor traffic.

Putney has largely escaped road widenings. It was long intended to widen the High Street, as the upper storeys of British Home Stores, set back from the street when rebuilt, bear witness, but the widening was never carried out. Proposals made in 1973 to deal with the High Street traffic, including a relief tunnel to its west which would have made it possible to pedestrianise part of the High Street, also came to nothing. The Greater London Council planned in 1965 to build a motorway through Putney, on the north side of the railway, as part of its plan for three orbital motorways around London, and the abandonment of these plans was one of the most important planning decisions affecting Putney since the war. Similar plans were revived in the late 1980s but were again abandoned. Roehampton has been less fortunate. Roehampton Lane from Fairacres to Rodway Road, previously a narrow lane between high brick walls, was widened in the late 1950s, and the section through the village, meeting the widened A3, in the mid-1960s.

122. The race to be first across the bridge without paying the toll, and the disposal of one of the toll gates (into the river!), July 1880.

123. The new bridge (before widening) and the District Railway bridge, c.1930.

124. Construction of the present Putney Bridge, about 1885. On the right is the old bridge, with the pipes from the Putney Heath reservoir diverted alongside it. On the left is one of the piers of the new bridge, and the old aqueduct converted into a track for cranes to run along.

125. Lower Richmond Road in 1910, with a variety of forms of transport.

126. Putney Heath, c.1880, with the Green Man in the background (watercolour by W.A. Nicholls).

Open spaces

WIMBLEDON AND PUTNEY COMMONS

Few areas of London are as fortunate as Putney in the amount of open space they enjoy, including Wimbledon Common and Putney Heath, Putney Lower Common and Richmond Park. Together with the River Thames they help to define Putney's boundaries and give it a sense of identity which is rare among London suburbs.

The Commons were often referred to as 'the waste of the manor', and were the parish's least fertile areas. They were not 'common lands' in the sense of being available for use by all residents. They were in the sole ownership of the lord of the manor, but people who held land as tenants of the manor (copyholders) had certain rights in them which meant that the lord of the manor could not treat the Commons as his private property.

Common rights were of three sorts. Grazing rights were sometimes varied but in the Tudor and Stuart period every holder of fifteen acres could graze five 'beasts for the plough' (originally oxen, but sometimes horses), 25 sheep and two pigs. Cottagers could turn out two cattle, one horse and one pig. Secondly, tenants could take wood for particular purposes, though not for sale: whole trees to make or repair their cottages, ploughs and carts, and smaller pieces of wood such as thorns, furze and the branches of pollard trees to use as firewood or for repairing hedges. The third right was to take gravel, sand or loam from the Common for their own use from designated pits.[1]

The manor court rolls, dating back to 1461, reveal the court's attempts to preserve the Commons from misuse. The commonest offences were exceeding one's rights to graze animals and to take wood. Examples from Edward IV's reign are Thomas West (father of Nicholas West) taking four cart-loads of thorns and underwood; Robert Sawyer cutting down four oaks without permission and making planks with them; John Hood overburdening 'Roehampton Common' with cattle; the Dean of St Paul's overburdening Putney Common with sheep, though not a tenant there; John Sanger putting eighty more sheep on Roehampton Common than he was entitled to; various people wrongfully putting animals on Putney Common, including twenty geese; and William Wight and his wife Isabella, who were not tenants, wrongfully gathering crab-apples and wildings.[2]

As a large, uncultivated space on which crowds could assemble, the Commons were also put to other uses. In May 1648, after the First Civil War, the men of Surrey, led by a Wandsworth miller, gathered on Putney Heath and marched to Westminster Hall to demand constitutional government by King and Par-

127. Wimbledon Common windmill, built in 1817 (engraving by George Cooke, 1825).

liament.[3] Thirteen years later the first parade of the Tangier Regiment of Foot took place on the Heath, at a site near Kingsmere now marked by a monument. Tangier had been given by Portugal to Britain as part of the dowry of Charles II's bride, Catherine of Braganza.

George III held several military reviews on the Common, which attracted huge crowds, and in 1811 the Prince Regent reviewed 28,000 Regulars and Volunteers there.[4] One of the last reviews was in 1891, when 22,000 troops paraded on the Common in the presence of the German Kaiser. Sometimes there were military manoeuvres, the last being in 1874, when 8,000 Surrey Volunteers staged such a realistic battle scene that several hundred acres of the Commons were severely damaged or set on fire.

The quietness and remoteness of the Commons made them a favourite place for duels, which were illegal. The Green Man was a popular base for duellers, the motto being 'pistols for two and breakfast for one'. The earliest recorded duel was between Lord Chandos and Colonel Henry Compton in May 1652, when Lord Chandos was killed. Compton and his second were later convicted of manslaughter. A sensational duel took place in 1789, between the Duke of York, who was next in line to the throne, and Colonel Lennox, a fellow officer in the Coldstream Guards, as the result of a political quarrel at a dinner party. Neither was hurt. Other well-known figures involved in duels included Lord Castlereagh, Secretary-at-War, and George Canning, Foreign Secretary, in 1809. In 1798 the Prime Minister, William Pitt, faced William Tierney, MP for Southwark. Both were so ignorant of firearms that no damage was done, but the fact that a Prime Minister had taken part in a duel was regarded as particularly shocking.

One of the last duels in England took place in 1841 between Lord Cardigan, an intensely quarrelsome man, who later led the Charge of the Light Brigade and gave his name to a popular garment, and a fellow officer, Captain Henry Tuckett, who was injured in the duel. The contest was witnessed from the Windmill by the miller, who was also the constable, and who arrested both parties. Lord Cardigan was subsequently tried by the House of Lords but acquitted.[5]

The Commons' quietness also attracted highwaymen. The most famous local highwayman was Jerry Abershaw, who generally operated from the Baldfaced Stag in Putney Vale. Like most highwaymen, he was brought to justice at an early age. In 1795, aged 23, after operating for about five years, he was hanged on Kennington Common, the place of execution for Surrey. His body was hung in chains near the scene of his crimes, at a place on the Heath still called Jerry's Hill.[6] Other people who took advantage of the Commons' quietness are indicated by an entry in the churchwardens' accounts in February 1747 for 'expences with the parish officers looking after the whores on Lovelands Hill, taking Betty Birch & puting the rest to flight'. Lovelands Hill appears to have been near the junction of Roehampton Lane and the present A3.[7]

In 1845, William Prosser was permitted to lay an experimental railway line on the Common to test his ideas. The line ran from Thatched Cottage to the Windmill, with a large turning circle north of the Windmill, the outline of which is still reflected in some footpaths. Its main features were the use of wooden rails instead of iron, and of small guide-wheels running against the inside faces of the track instead of flanges to keep the train on the rails. His ideas won some support, but were never adopted.

128. A drawing by George Cruikshank of the duel between Canning and Castlereagh in 1809.

129. *Prosser's railway, 1845.*

THE PRESERVATION OF THE COMMONS

The Commons have from time to time been reduced in area by enclosures. Some of these have already been noted: the new fields of the thirteenth century, the Pightles in the mid-fifteenth century and the new village at Roehampton, chiefly of the seventeenth century. Sometimes these were unauthorised and contested, but at least as often the enclosure was authorised by the lord of the manor and the manorial tenants and a payment was made to the lord. The most drastic attempt at enclosure prior to the nineteenth century took place when Edward Ferrers, lessee of Barn Elms, sought to enclose both Barnes Common and Putney Lower Common in 1627-8, provoking riots in which his fences were thrown down. On being petitioned by local people, Charles I appointed two privy councillors to investigate. They found that the enclosure was 'vexing and impoverishing...manie poore laboring men there wifes and children', and ordered Ferrers to leave the Commons open.[8]

From the 1760s to the first decade of the nineteenth century substantial areas were enclosed with the agreement of the lord of the manor and the tenants and were used for building or for extending the grounds of large houses.[9] They included land around the former bowling green on the Heath, along the northern edge of the Heath, and on and around the Lower Common (for example the site later used for Putney Hospital). Subsequent enclosures were usually for public purposes, but became increasingly numerous - extra land for the telegraph in 1821, schools at Roehampton in 1836 and 1854, the reservoir on Putney Heath in 1852, All Saints School in 1858, the cemetery on the Lower Common in 1858, and All Saints Church in 1870, the latter isolating a small patch of common land which now forms the Erpingham Road tennis courts. In the nineteenth century the Commons were more vulnerable to large-scale enclosure than ever before. The number of copyholders exercising their common rights had declined, while the increasing local population and building activity exacerbated problems such as the taking of gravel and clay and the dumping of rubbish; it also gave the Commons value as building land. Parts of the Common near Roehampton village were said to be 'in a deplorable state of devastation' in 1837, with night soil and the emptyings of pig-sties being dumped there.[10] Gypsies were another problem: the minister at Roehampton accused them in 1864 of 'things so atrocious that it had been impossible to put them on paper'. On the other hand, there was a growing number of suburban residents with a strong interest in the attractiveness and recreational value of the Commons.

The crisis came in 1864, when the lord of the manor, the fifth Earl Spencer, called a meeting in the Wimbledon Village Club. The object of the meeting had not been stated and attendance was small, but fortunately

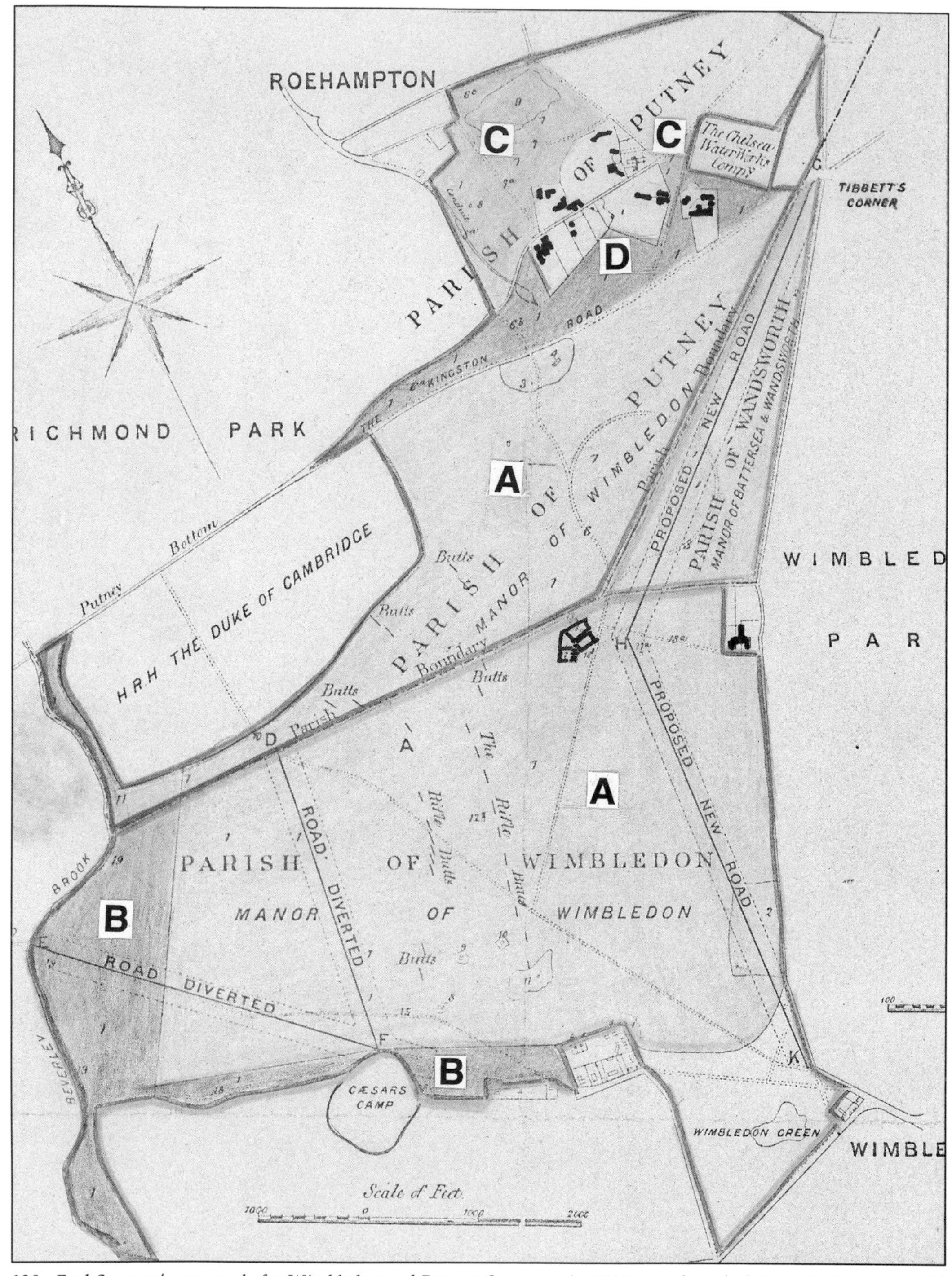

130. *Earl Spencer's proposals for Wimbledon and Putney Commons in 1864. Land marked A was to become a public park; B was to be sold to cover the costs; C was also to be sold if the proceeds of A were insufficient; and D was to be sold if the proceeds of B and C were insufficient.*

Henry Peek of Wimbledon House had sent a shorthand-writer, and later published Earl Spencer's proposals. His Lordship had decided that Wimbledon Common had become unmanageable. He emphasised the evils of lack of drainage, rubbish dumping and gypsy encampments. He was therefore seeking powers in a parliamentary bill to enclose 700 acres of Wimbledon and Putney Commons as a public park, and to sell parts of the remaining 300 acres to cover the costs. Depending on the level of costs, most of Putney Heath north of the present A3 could have been enclosed. Up to two acres was to be allocated for a new manor house on the site of the Windmill.

The majority of those present were in favour of the proposals, but under the strong influence of Henry Peek committees were formed in Wimbledon and Putney to oppose them. These committees found powerful allies, for the threat to build on Putney Heath had given rise to a parliamentary committee which was inquiring into the best way to preserve the commons near London. This resulted in the Metropolitan Commons Act of 1866 and also the birth of the Commons Preservation Society, still active (as the Open Spaces Society) more than a century later. Meanwhile, Earl Spencer had withdrawn his Bill, but an armed truce continued for some years while both sides investigated their legal rights. Spencer asserted his right to absolute ownership by opening a brickfield and brick kiln, digging turf and gravel and agreeing to lease land for a sewage works and he also bought up copyhold properties under false names to extinguish their common rights.

131. Sir Henry Peek, who led the opposition to the enclosure of the Commons.

In 1870 it became clear that Spencer was ready to come to terms, and the result, after difficult negotiations, was the Wimbledon and Putney Commons Act, which received Royal Assent in August 1871. The Act covered Putney Lower Common, which had not been included in Earl Spencer's original scheme.

The Act provided that Earl Spencer's rights in the Commons should be bought out by an annual payment of £1200, this being the average amount he had derived from them over the previous ten years. The Commons were to be vested in a body of eight Conservators, of whom three would be appointed by Ministers of the Crown (now the Home Secretary and the Secretaries of State for Defence and the Environment) and the other five would be elected by local residents every three years, the latter being thus assured of a majority.

To pay for Earl Spencer's annuity and for the upkeep of the Commons, the Conservators were empowered to levy a rate on all occupiers of residential property over a certain value within ¾ mile walking distance over public roads of Wimbledon Common or beyond that distance in the parish of Putney: the amounts were based on rateable value and the distance of the property from the Common. This system remains in force, apart from changes resulting from the abolition of local authority rates, and it is this local control over the Commons which has enabled them to survive. The annuity to Earl Spencer, which had passed into the hands of an insurance company, was paid off in 1968.

THE COMMONS UNDER THE CONSERVATORS

The first Conservators were faced with some difficult problems. First there was the task of ending some of the abuses which had sparked off the crisis, such as the gravel-digging. The Lower Common suffered at the hands of a 'somewhat low and rough set of people who had been in the habit of misusing it'. Cows, donkeys, geese and pigs roamed on it, and sewage from dairies and piggeries made its north-east corner 'a stinking swamp'. Carts were left around, rubbish was dumped, and washerwomen put out their clothes to dry. Some possible rights were bought out, such as those of Mrs Morrison to turn her geese onto the Common; she was paid £5.[11]

Another problem was that the championships of the National Rifle Association (NRA) took place on the Common for a fortnight each July, attracting great numbers of people, with a large area enclosed for the event. These contests, begun in 1860, now had the formal sanction of the 1871 Act. Certain restrictions were imposed by the Act, but the Camp grew each year, and the ancillary buildings became more nu-

132. The gatekeeper's cottage at the boundary between Barnes Common and Putney Lower Common (engraving by Clough Bromley).

133. National Rifle Association camp on the Putney side of the windmill, c.1880.

134. Richardson Evans, who promoted the extension of the Commons, enabling the playing fields between Beverley Brook and Putney Vale Estate to be added.

merous. Relations between the NRA and the Conservators were 'co-operative, if not cordial', and various improvements, such as drainage and road-making, were paid for by the NRA. Eventually the increasing power and range of the rifle, and the growth in residential property round the Common, made the ranges unsafe, and in 1890 they were moved to Bisley.

As the abuses were checked, and particularly once the NRA departed, the task could begin of making the Commons fit for their new role of public recreation. This involved tree-planting, drainage, new rides and footpaths and levelling. The levelling may have gone too far, especially around the turn of the century when spoil from the construction of underground railways was deposited on the Lower Common and its whole aspect was changed. Generous provision was made for cricket and football. Queensmere was formed in 1887 by damming a stream.

Just before the First World War the efforts of Mr Richardson Evans and the public support given to his Commons Extension Scheme enabled 175 acres, including much of Newlands Farm west of Putney Vale Estate, to be added to the Common. The Richardson Evans Memorial Playing Fields were subsequently laid out there.

The most recent threat to the Commons has been the taking of land for road widening, especially at Tibbets Corner. With difficulty the Conservators were able to obtain land of equal extent in compensation, and this included a riverside walk along Beverley Brook to the Thames.

RICHMOND PARK

More of Richmond Park is in Putney Parish than in Richmond Parish (237 acres compared with 69). Charles I created the Park in the 1630s, in the face of strong local opposition and deep disquiet among his closest advisers. It is thought to have substantially increased his unpopularity, especially as he started to build the enormously expensive enclosing wall before all those having lands within it had agreed to sell. Much of this wall is still standing. Most of the Roehampton land was taken from the Earl of Portland's newly-created Roehampton Park, though some was common land.[12]

Charles I was passionately fond of hunting and his object was to acquire a more spacious area for his sport than his existing parks at Richmond and Hampton Court could provide. The Park was ready for use by June 1637, and from then until the outbreak of the Civil War five years later the King made full use of it. Putney's church bells were rung twice in April 1635 'when ye kinge and Prince Ellector cam over to the New Parke to see his deare', and thirteen times in 1638-9 'the King & Queene coming through the towne to goe to ye New Parke & to Richmont'.[13]

After the execution of Charles I in 1649 and the confiscation of the royal estates, Parliament gave Richmond Park to the City of London with the intention that it be preserved as a park and remain an 'ornament to the City'. On the Restoration of the monarchy in 1660 the City prudently restored it to the new King, and the Park has never again been out of royal ownership. Deer hunting remained the Park's main purpose until the mid-eighteenth century, after which the emphasis shifted to the provision of large quantities of venison for distribution by royal warrant. In the eighteenth century the limited public access which Charles I had reluctantly conceded began to be restricted, and when George II's daughter Princess Amelia was appointed Ranger in 1751 she stopped it altogether. This caused considerable protest and was contested in the courts by John Lewis, a Richmond brewer, who based his case on the rights of access permitted by Charles I. Lewis won the case and access for pedestrians was restored. Even so, until the mid-nineteenth century pedestrians appear to have been largely confined to the roads and footpaths, and access remained restricted until the beginning of the present century.[14] Most of the Roehampton lands lying east of Beverley Brook have never been open to the public. They have been used for a variety of purposes, principally for paddocking of deer and the growing of hay for their fodder; also for grazing sheep, which have sometimes been kept in the Park. In recent years ten acres have been used as a hayfield, and eight for the Hyde Park Nursery. Kingsfarm Lodge marks what had been the Ranger's Farm but became King's Farm when George III became Ranger.[15]

The one gate within Putney Parish – Roehampton Gate – was unusual in that it opened onto private property. This was probably because Jerome Weston, the second Earl of Portland, whose land it was, was the first Keeper (or Ranger) of the Park. The owner of the private road leading from Roehampton Gate to Roehampton was later among those entitled to venison from the Park.

OTHER OPEN SPACES

Putney has few small parks and gardens. A strip of land north of the Lower Richmond Road, between Pentlow and Danemere Streets, originated as an entrance way to Barn Elms, on the opposite side of Beverley Brook. Leader's Gardens, 2½ acres by the river, takes its name from John Temple Leader, a major landowner and developer, who had a house on Putney Hill, though he lived for his lat fifty years in a castle near Florence. It was opened in 1903, the year of Leader's death, and enlarged by Wandsworth Borough Council in the late 1970s by taking in part of Ashlone Road and the old borough depot beside the Creek. The whole riverside can, of course, be regarded as one of Putney's finest open spaces.

Otherwise there is only the Old Burial Ground beside Putney Police Station, given to the parish in 1763 by the Revd Roger Pettiward and closed in 1854. By the 1960s it had become derelict but it was then tidied and re-arranged as a public garden.

135. 'Maying on Putney Heath', c.1907.

Rowing

By 1872, a witness seeking to justify a new railway to Putney could describe it as 'the metropolis of the rowing world'.[1] Putney's ascendancy in amateur rowing was then fairly recent, as was amateur rowing itself, but there had been rowing by professionals for much longer, both at Putney and elsewhere. The first annual race, Doggett's Coat and Badge, was founded in 1715 by an Irish actor and theatre manager, Thomas Doggett, for young watermen just out of their seven years' apprenticeship. Although the race was from London Bridge to Chelsea (at first against the tide and taking nearly two hours), and did not come as far as Putney, there have been more winners from Putney than from any other stretch of the river, including eight members of the Phelps family between 1884 and 1938.[2] No riverside event is now complete without a few Doggett's winners resplendent in their scarlet coats and silver badges.

Professional rowing reached its peak in the mid-nineteenth century, with a huge public following, and much of this activity was at Putney. The present university boat race course was used for the professional sculling championship of England before the university crews adopted it.[3] The professional races

137. Six members of the Phelps family who won Doggett's Coat and Badge. C. Phelps (middle of front row, winner in 1884) was the grandfather of E.H. Phelps (middle of back row, winner in 1938) and the father of the other four. The images of C. and E.H. Phelps were 'ghosted in' to a photograph of the four brothers.

136. The Royal Thames National Regatta in 1856. In the background is the newly-constructed aqueduct.

138. The Regatta Fair on the towpath at Putney, 1846.

were rowdier events than their amateur counterparts, with large wagers and much fouling. By the 1880s, however, professional rowing was in decline, partly because of competing sports with greater spectator appeal, and some of the later races and prizes at Putney were an attempt to revive it. The London Rowing Club of Putney instituted a London Coat and Badge in 1875, their coat being of blue velvet. This continued until 1905, and was revived as the Putney Coat and Badge in 1911. The last race was in 1925, when it was won by E.A. Phelps.[4]

Organised amateur rowing began in a significant way only in the 1820s and 1830s, and its chief centres were Oxford, Cambridge and the metropolitan Thames, especially Putney. Putney achieved its unique position because further downstream the Thames was now usually too crowded (and probably also too polluted) for rowing. In the 1830s there was only a single boathouse at Putney,[5] and it was in the 1850s that amateur rowing became firmly established and well-organised. The London Rowing Club, Putney's first, was founded in 1856 with the aim of establishing a large membership for a low subscription. Its headquarters were at the Star and Garter until it built its present boathouse in 1871. The Amateur Rowing Association (originally the National Rowing Association) has been based at the Club since its formation in 1882. The Thames Rowing Club was founded in 1861, less for competitive rowing than to provide pleasure boating for clerks and salesmen of the London drapery warehouses and similar institutions, although its social status had risen by the 1870s.[6] Its boathouse dates from 1879.

The Leander Club, the oldest on the Thames, was based at Putney from 1860 to 1896, when its headquarters moved to Henley, though it kept its boathouse at Putney until 1939. Vesta moved from Wands-

139. The boathouses and towpath in 1878, before construction of the Embankment. On the left is the London Rowing Club's boathouse.

140. Searle & Sons, 1851. Their premises were later occupied by Ayling.

141. The boat-building workshop of E. Ayling & Sons, between Ruvigny Gardens and the Embankment, c.1900.

142. *Edmund Norris, manufacturer of oars and sculls, on the Embankment between Rotherwood and Festing Roads. Norris moved to this building, which still exists, in about 1900, and remained in business there until the Second World War.*

143. *E. Ayling & Sons, c.1900. A notice to the right announces the intended erection of flats (now Ruvigny Mansions).*

worth to Putney in about 1873, and to its present quarters by Rotherwood Road (subsequently rebuilt) in 1890. Putney Rowing Club followed in 1888. Sailing arrived with the establishment of the Ranelagh Sailing Club in 1889.[7]

The rise of rowing gave a new lease of life to Putney's watermen, and some, notably the Phelpses, were able to combine rowing with boatbuilding, coaching or acting as boatman to amateur clubs. Riverside inns such as the Star and Garter also took full advantage of the new sport. Boatbuilding, which dates back to the seventeenth century in Putney, flourished. Since 1937 almost all the boats for the university boat race have been provided by the Sims family of Putney and Hammersmith. Also on the Embankment were Ayling & Sons, oar and scull makers, which originated in the Vauxhall area in 1852 and moved to Putney in about 1900. Since 1869 the firm has supplied the oars for the Oxford and Cambridge boats, but it is no longer based at Putney.

THE OXFORD AND CAMBRIDGE BOAT RACE

The event for which Putney is famous is the annual Boat Race between Oxford and Cambridge universities. The first race, in 1829, took place at Henley, and the next five were from Westminster to Putney. The present 4¼ mile course was adopted in 1845, although on three occasions (the last in 1863) it has been rowed from Mortlake to Putney. The event has been annual since 1856, except for 1915-19 and 1940-5.[8]

Professional watermen were used at first to coach and direct the crews. In 1877 one of them, 'Honest John Phelps', aged over 70, was to judge the result. It was an extremely close race, and there were then no finishing posts. According to a hostile observer, Phelps called out 'Dead heat to Oxford by five feet'. A supporter of Phelps wrote later that Phelps' eyesight had simply been too poor to see the result. It was the only dead heat in the race's history, and the last time that professional watermen were involved.

The race did not at first attract much attention. According to Charles Dickens junior,

> The comparatively few people who watched the practice of the crews all seemed to know each other...Past University oarsmen, their jerseys exchanged for the decorous high waistcoat, the white choker taking the place of the rowing man's muffler, were to be met all over Putney, and about Searle's yard and the London Boat-house. The towing-path was a sort of Rialto or High 'Change, on which old friends met and renewed their youth as they talked over old times and criticised their successors. There were but few rowing-clubs then; the river had not become the fashion.[9]

However, by the 1880s the race had captured the

144. The finish of the 1846 University Boat Race at Putney. This was the first race over the present course, and one of three rowed from Mortlake to Putney. Plumes of smoke rise from steamboats and paddlesteamers in the background.

public imagination and was attracting huge crowds. There were festivities for two weeks while the crews practised, and a local resident recorded how 'the light and dark blue flags of the rival universities float gracefully from the houses and gardens of their respective partisans'.[10] Entertainers of all kinds amused the crowds, and children chanted defiant jingles, of which 'Cambridge upstairs putting on their braces; Oxford downstairs winning all the races' (or vice versa) is a fair example. In the 1880s Charles Dickens junior wrote disapprovingly that

> Cabmen, butcher boys and omnibus drivers sport the colours of the universities in all directions: the dark blue of Oxford and the light blue of Cambridge fill all the hosiers' shops, and are flaunted in all sorts of indescribable company. Every publican who has a flag-staff hoists a flag to mark his preference and to show which way his crown or so has gone...Everybody talks about the race, and it generally happens that the more ignorant of the matter is the company the more heated the discussion, and the more confident and dogmatic the opinions expressed.

He believed that the race had become 'the centre of the most undesirable surroundings' and should be moved further away from London.[11]

Prior to radio and television, newsboys would squat over their papers, feverishly inserting the result in the stop-press column with rubber stamps, and the result was painted up on the great staircase (now destroyed) in W.H. Smith's shop in the High Street. A running commentary was broadcast on the radio for the first time in 1927; television followed in 1938 and from 1949 to the present. Radio and television and competing attractions have reduced the race's glamour, but it can still bring out the crowds in their thousands.

OTHER EVENTS

The Wingfield Sculls, now the British Amateur Sculling Championship, began in 1830, as a sort of amateur version of Doggett's Coat and Badge. From 1849 it was rowed from Putney to Kew, and in 1861 the present course from Putney to Mortlake was adopted.

The Metropolitan Amateur Regatta was started at Putney in 1866, providing prizes for eights, fours and scullers. Its course has varied, but in recent years has been from the University Stone in Putney to Harrods Wharf or from Hammersmith Bridge to the London Rowing Club flagstaff, according to the tide. It lasts for three evenings.

145. The 1870 Boat Race, with old Putney Bridge in the foreground and the two crews about to pass Hammersmith Bridge.

Putney Town Regatta was first held in 1911.[12] For a time it formed part of 'Putney Week', which included swimming events and attractions such as 'climbing the greasy pole', and culminated in a splendid fireworks display in Bishop's Park. Today the Regatta continues, but, shorn of its fireworks, is now a more serious sporting occasion.

The annual Head of the River race, for eights, was started in 1926 to encourage rowing in winter. It is rowed on the ebb tide from Mortlake to Putney. There were 21 starters in the first race, but it now attracts over 400 crews and is the most spectacular of Putney's rowing events.[13]

146. The Eight Bells, on the riverside near the aqueduct, 1881. This was where the towpath towards Kew began.

Putney at Play

PUBS

The earliest known alehouses and inns were at the bottom of Putney High Street near the ferry landing, where they catered for thirsty travellers as well as locals. The Red Lion, which existed from the fifteenth century until about 1887, was the most prominent, and was an important meeting place, sometimes accommodating the manor court, as well as being the venue for the annual parochial dinner. Immediately south of it in 1617 were two lesser inns, the White Lion and the Bull, and nearby on the same side of the street were the Falcon, the Lord of Exeter's Arms and the Queens Arms. The only survivors from that period (both rebuilt) are the White Lion (currently the Slug and Lettuce) and the Anchor (now the Fox and Hounds).[1] In Roehampton, all the public houses recorded prior to the eighteenth century were in the old village in Roehampton Lane, except for the Half Way House or Baldfaced Stag in Putney Vale, established in about 1650;[2] none of these survives.

In 1786, when the continuous series of licensing records begins, there were 15 public houses in Putney and three in Roehampton. One – the Sugar Loaves, in the Ruvigny Gardens area – disappeared in 1787, possibly the result of a local campaign against disorderly alehouses which encouraged 'vice, lewdness, profaneness and immorality'. Otherwise, the same 17 pubs continued until 1830, and no others date back before then.[3] Ten of the 17 survive today, though their premises have mostly been rebuilt. They are the Castle, the Dukes Head, the Fox and Hounds, the Green Man, the Half Moon, the Spotted Horse, the Star and Garter and the White Lion; and in Roehampton, the Angel and the Kings Head.

Among the seven which have disappeared were the Eight Bells by the waterside, the Rose and Crown adjacent to the church gate (suppressed as a nuisance in 1887), the Bull and Star in the High Street (closed in 1971) and the Baldfaced Stag at Roehampton. In the 1680s the landlord of the latter looked after horses used by Charles II and his courtiers for hunting in Richmond Park.[4]

Of the survivors from 1786, most seem to have originated earlier in the same century, despite the

147. *The Spotted Horse, decorated for Queen Victoria's Jubilee (1887 or 1897).*

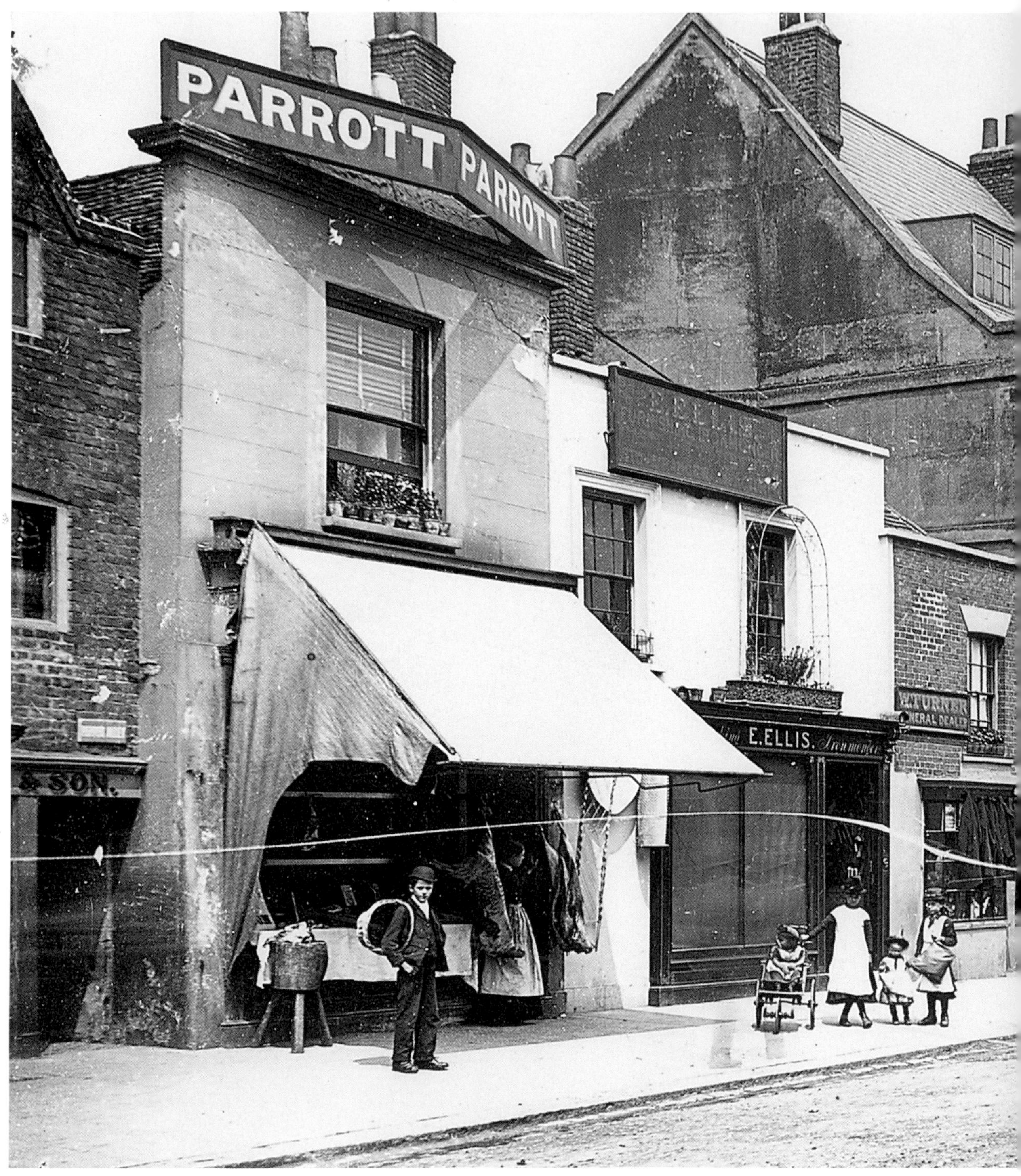

148. The west side of Putney High Street, c.1880, seen from between Felsham and Lacy Roads. The original Bull and Star occupied two-thirds of the large building with the sloping roof on the corner of Felsham Road.

YOUNG &
BAINBRIDGES
TO THE
BREWERY
FURNITURE WAREHOUSE.
HOUSE FURNISHER.
WAREHOUSE
KAIN

149. A room at the Kings Head, Roehampton, in 1901.

150. The Castle, on the corner of Putney Bridge Road and Brewhouse Lane, c.1880. The photographer is looking east along Putney Bridge Road.

151. The Half Moon, prior to its rebuilding in about 1904.

claims of much greater antiquity sometimes made. The Castle has often been described as the birthplace of Thomas Cromwell, Henry VIII's chief minister, but although his father Walter apparently owned the brewery at the other end of Brewhouse Lane,[5] no direct link with the Castle has been demonstrated, and the Castle is not recorded as a pub name until the eighteenth century. Its present building was put up in 1959. The Green Man dates from the early eighteenth century, and almost certainly retains its original building.[6] It was long associated with duels which took place on the Heath. The Half Moon also originated in the early eighteenth century. It served some of the poorest areas of Putney, and was often in trouble with the licensing authorities.[7] The Spotted Horse has an antique appearance which in fact dates from the twentieth century, but underneath the ornamentation is an eighteenth or early nineteenth-century cottage. In Roehampton, the Kings Head may be the oldest secular building remaining in the borough, parts of it dating back at least to the 1670s, but it is not recorded as a pub until the 1720s, when it was known as the Bull.[8]

Licensing regulations were relaxed by the Beer Act of 1830, under which anyone could turn their house into a beer shop without the need for a licence. Many

152. The Green Man, c.1910.

153. The original Quill public house: an outing about to begin. Probably about 1910.

of Putney's present pubs originated in this way. Those recorded in the 1830s are the Jolly Gardeners and the Bricklayers Arms; the Telegraph (named after the Admiralty's semaphore station) appeared in 1844. The Bricklayers Arms retains its original premises (the only survivor from River Street), and so does the Montague Arms in Roehampton, a mid-eighteenth century cottage which became a beer shop in the 1860s. However, most of the beer shops which succeeded in obtaining a licence after the regulations were tightened again have been rebuilt on a grander scale, including the Cricketers, the Spencer Arms and the Coat and Badge. Some other pubs started as beer shops but were clearly intended from the start as full public houses, including the Arab Boy (1849), the Quill (1854) and the Railway Hotel (1857). The first two of these were built by Henry Scarth in connection with his housing developments in Putney. The quill was that of his father, who had used it as a solicitor to build the family fortunes, while the Arab boy was his servant, Yussef Sirrie, whom he had brought back with him from travels overseas. The original Arab Boy remains, but the present Quill dates only from 1964.[9]

Other present-day pubs appeared during the main period of suburban development, and include the Northumberland Arms, the Cedar Tree, the Prince of Wales and, in Roehampton, the Earl Spencer. The number of pubs did not, however, keep pace with the population. In 1786 there was about one per 125 inhabitants, in 1830 about one per 225, and in 1871 about one per 375. Pubs therefore became larger. Most were rebuilt in the late nineteenth century, including the White Lion (1887), the Angel (1892-3), the Spencer Arms (1898), the Star and Garter (1900), and the Half Moon (by 1904). More recently, there have been a few new pubs to serve the new housing estates, including the Ranger on the Ashburton Estate (a reference to the Ranger in charge of Wimbledon and Putney Commons), the Maltese Cat in Aubyn Square (named after a famous polo pony) and the Highwayman in Petersfield Rise.

Pubs were not of course solely for drinking in. Skittle grounds were to be found at the Angel and the Spotted Horse (and no doubt others) in the late nineteenth century. Riverside pubs such as the Star and Garter provided boathouses. And pubs were among the few places which could offer meeting rooms, such as the 'club rooms' at the Castle and the Dukes Head.[10]

154. The Thames Rowing Club's athletics in Putney Park in 1869.

SPORTS AND RECREATION

The first organised recreation recorded was a bowling alley in a field west of Walkers Place in 1617. By 1636 there was a much more important bowling green on Putney Heath (adjoining the Portsmouth Road), which became a fashionable place for public breakfasts and evening assemblies. It was also where the Surrey Justices of the Peace held their monthly meetings in the late seventeenth century. A second green was added in 1707, but bowling lost popularity in the eighteenth century, and the last of the two greens closed in about 1770, when Bowling Green House became a private residence. The site is now marked by Bowling Green Close and Heathview Gardens. The present public bowling green on the Lower Common, dating from 1935, replaced one provided in 1912 by Sir William Lancaster, over which Putney Hospital had been extended.[11]

Horse riding took place on the Common. When Samuel Pepys called on Sir William Coventry in May 1667 the latter had gone to Putney Heath to run some horses with the King and the Duke of York. In the early eighteenth century there were annual horse races on the Common. There was also hunting: the Queen's Buck Hounds were recorded on Putney Heath in 1706.[12]

155. The Thames Hare and Hounds at 'Roehampton Bottom' in 1869.

Cricket has a long history in Putney. A match between Putney and Fulham took place on Putney Heath in 1730.[13] In 1800 the manor court heard complaints that 'divers persons frequently play at cricket on Putney Lower Common, near the gate leading from Windsor Street to Barnes, to the great inconvenience and annoyance of travellers passing and re-passing, by the cricket-balls being flung in the road, and the players stopping them with their batts in an improper manner, to the obstruction of horses in

156. Putney Embankment, c.1930.

157. The towpath bridge over Beverley Brook.

carriages'.[14] In 1857 a local resident complained that it was 'quite impossible to play a *quiet* match there in consequence of all the worst of Putney making a point of attending it; what with the music, the yelling, quoits, "knock em downs" &c it made our usually comparatively quiet Common more like Greenwich Fair or the Course at Epsom than anything else'; he thought the cricket was 'got up for selling beer'.[15] Not for nothing is there a nearby pub called the Cricketers.

Another place associated with cricket was Half Moon Fields, stretching down from the pub of that name to the river. It seems to have become the town's main recreation ground in the nineteenth century, until submerged under Bendemeer and other roads. On Easter Monday 1887, for example, the 'fete and gala' there consisted of a 'grand cricket match (Putney Ramblers v Tunbridge Wells), stage performances, dancing al fresco, concluding with a grand display of fireworks'.[16]

Of the existing cricket clubs, Roehampton Cricket Club was formed in 1842 and was allowed its present pitch on Putney Heath by Lord Spencer in 1859. Putney Cricket Club, at first known as St John's, followed in 1870, with a pitch on the Lower Common. Within a few years of the establishment of the Commons Conservators in 1871 there were three cricket clubs using the Lower Common. More pitches were made available there by diverting a road and levelling the ground. A number of the large houses around Putney Heath had their own cricket grounds and fielded their own house teams.[17]

Out of rowing came a sport in which Putney can claim an undisputed world first – cross-country running. The first ever cross-country race, other than the paper-chases of schoolboys, was organised by Thames Rowing Club as winter training for its crews. This developed into the Thames Hare and Hounds. The first race, the 'Thames Handicap Steeplechase No. 1', took place on 17 October 1868 from the Kings Head in Roehampton. The organiser, Walter Rye, had drawn his inspiration from the Barby Hill run in *Tom Brown's Schooldays*.[18] Cross-country running has continued on the Common ever since.

Tennis arrived in Putney in 1879 with the formation of the Putney Lawn Tennis Club, within a few years of the invention of lawn tennis in 1873. Founded as a 'lawn tennis and archery club', its first ground was on the northern corner of Gwendolen and St John's Avenues; it moved in 1891 to a site in Howards Lane, on which Tideswell Road was later built, and finally in 1904 to its present home in Balmuir Gardens. It had some of the earliest hard courts in the world, and produced a number of world-famous players.[19]

Focusing only on organised sports would give a distorted picture, especially as regards local children. In 1884, for example, the Vestry complained about 'the assembling of gangs of boys on Sundays for tossing &c' on a piece of land between Lacy Road and Felsham Road. The police replied that 'a large number of children assemble there daily and use the spot as a playground. Gambling does not take place, but boys play at marbles, buttons, tip-cat, &c', adding that 'were the children driven from the spot they would only become a nuisance in the streets'.[20]

Severe winters saw skaters flocking to any suitable stretch of ice. For example, the 'Rally Pond' by Queen's Ride Bridge attracted skaters from long distances. There was a 'curling pond' a little west of Kingsmere. At one time the Thames itself occasionally froze over, and in January 1789 there was a fair on the river upstream from the bridge, with puppet shows and roundabouts; according to a contemporary newspaper, 'Putney and Fulham, from morning dawn to the dusk of returning evening, are a scene of festivity and gaiety'. The last great frost was in 1881.[21]

Swimming was popular when the river was cleaner. In 1660 it was reported that Charles II and the future James II 'come every evening as far as Battersea, Putney and Barn Elms to swim and bathe themselves, and take great delight in it and swim excellent well'.[22] Professional swimming championships were later contested in the Thames at Putney, and the 1889 edition of Baedeker's *London* records that 'the races are swum in university costume and may be witnessed by ladies'. There were still swimming races in the river in 1922. An open air swimming pool was provided at Priory Lane, Roehampton, in the 1930s.[23]

Putney participated fully in the great days of cycling. The Velodrome, opened in 1892, was between Hotham Road and Clarendon Drive, and was the first cement cycling track in England. It was banked at both ends, and measured four and a half laps to the mile. Though rather small, it boasted at one time more records than any other track in England, and attracted crowds of up to 8000. It was also the headquarters of the Putney Athletic Club, and had facilities for tennis and bowls. However, the lease ran out in 1906, and the track moved to Herne Hill. Landford and Earldom Roads were built on the site.[24]

158. The Velodrome, c.1900

159. Ice skating on Kingsmere in about 1910.

Roehampton Club was formed in 1901-2 by a syndicate of polo players.[25] Though polo is no longer played, it continues to offer golf and other sports.

Golf for the ordinary man or woman did not come to the area until 1923, when George V gave approval for an 'artisans' golf course' on the eastern side of Richmond Park, available to all on payment of the green fee. Opened by the future Edward VIII and known as the Prince's Course, it was so popular that a second course was constructed and opened two years later by the Duke of York, becoming the Duke's Course.[26]

Putney has never been the home of a top football club, but it did acquire a first-class rugby club in 1957, when Rosslyn Park moved from Richmond to a ground leased from Roehampton Club in the Upper Richmond Road.[27]

Local inhabitants have derived pleasure and recreation from their gardens for centuries, and Roehampton Garden Society, founded in 1873 as the Roehampton Horticultural Society, is one of the oldest organisations in the area.

160. Title page of The Putney Bus, *probably of the 1870s. The song is about a man following a pretty woman, who takes the Putney bus. Eventually he discovers that she is his wife, and makes himself scarce.*

INDOOR ENTERTAINMENTS

Indoor swimming baths were opened by William Bishop in 1886 in Putney Bridge Road, at the corner of Burstock Road. They were advertised as 'hot, swimming and Turkish baths'. They closed in 1913,[28] the Council having refused to buy them, but the building survived until 1986. After 1913 there was no indoor swimming at Putney until the new swimming baths (now known as Putney Leisure Centre) were opened at Dryburgh Road in 1968.

The Assembly Rooms in Putney High Street date from the late 1870s, and have formed W.H. Smith's since 1922, though the spacious and elegant layout, with its double staircase, has been destroyed. They were used for meetings and concerts. It was probably in the Assembly Rooms that Putney's first public film-shows were given.[29] A small building in the Platt, later the works of the Cossentine Bolt Co., could be regarded as Putney's first cinema, since William Friese-Green (1855-1921), a pioneer of motion pictures, had demonstrated his films there, but this was probably not a public entertainment.[30]

Putney's first purpose-built cinemas opened in 1911. One was the Globe Cinema in the Upper Richmond Road (originally the Putney Electric Palace). It long maintained a very independent existence under a Welshman, Mr Rees Thomas Davies, and enjoyed a discerning clientele for its classic and foreign films.[31] It became the Cinecenta in the 1960s, losing its distinctive oriental facade in the process, and was demolished in 1976. The tiny Mirror Picture Theatre at the corner of Putney Bridge Road and Brewhouse Lane (advertised as 'the most cosy hall in the district') also

161. The Mirror Picture Theatre in Putney Bridge Road, c.1913. Behind it is the Castle.

162. The Globe Cinema, Upper Richmond Road (next to the Fox and Hounds), c.1920.

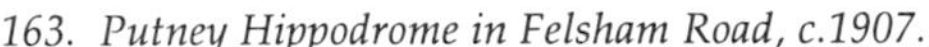

163. Putney Hippodrome in Felsham Road, c.1907.

opened in 1911, but lasted only until 1914,[32] although the building survived until 1971.

The grander Electric Picture Palace, almost on the corner of Putney Bridge Road and the High Street, also opened in about 1911. It changed owners and name frequently, ending its days as the Odeon. It was joined in 1937 by the huge Regal, later the A.B.C., on the adjacent site, capable of seating 2,500. Both were demolished in 1971 and replaced by a new cinema complex.

Putney's only purpose-built music hall was the Hippodrome in Felsham Road, opened in 1906 as the Putney Empire and Palace of Varieties. Many famous artistes appeared there, including Marie Lloyd, Vesta Tilley and Harry Champion. But the films defeated it, and it became a cinema in 1924. After closure in 1961 it lay empty for many years, during which it was used to make a horror film set in a derelict theatre. It was finally demolished in 1976. Putney has, however, since the 1960s possessed a theatre – the Goodrich Theatre in the Upper Richmond Road, where Group 64 performs.

165. The Electric Picture Palace (later the Odeon) at the lower end of Putney High Street, in about 1913.

164. The Regal Cinema, Putney High Street, 1937.

166. St Mary's Church, 1809. The external stairs led to a gallery which was lit by the dormer window. In front of the church is the toll house of the bridge.

Putney at Prayer

Until the nineteenth century it was only religion which regularly brought together a significant proportion of the local community. Even in the Victorian age, the churches were by far the largest local organisations and the biggest crowd-pullers, and they were heavily involved in education and welfare activities.

Up to the late eighteenth century, St Mary's was the only place of worship in Putney. From 1622 its care and maintenance is catalogued in immense detail in the churchwardens' accounts, right down to items such as one shilling to 'oulde father Paine for whipping dooges out of ye church on Sondaies in service tyme & for a whipp for him' in 1623.[1] Several notable ministers have served in it, such as Edward Sclater, who became a Roman Catholic in 1685 and was allowed by James II to retain his curacy and his school. Catholic priests were sent to his house and said mass there daily, but he found them very unsatisfactory: 'they would spend hours every day upon wavering Protestants, but scarce catechise children once a fortnight', and they insisted on knowing about everything said or done in his family. His wife complained about unintelligible services in Latin. Sclater recanted after the Catholic monarch was deposed in 1688.[2] Daniel Lysons, deputy curate from 1791 to 1799, wrote *The Environs of London* (1792-6), a classic of local history, notable for its use of

167. Daniel Lysons (1762-1834), deputy curate of Putney 1791-9.

168. The interior of old St Mary's, looking west. Bishop West's Chapel is on the left.

primary sources. During the Reformation, the right of patronage or appointment in the parish of Wimbledon (including Putney) was granted by Henry VIII to the Dean and Chapter of Worcester, who have retained it to the present day.

As Putney's population expanded, St Mary's was gradually enlarged, chiefly by adding galleries. As early as 1788, however, it was noted that 'many respectable families cannot attend for want of pews'.[3] The church was at last rebuilt in 1836, and only part of the arcading, the tower, several monuments and Bishop West's Chapel survive from the earlier building. The architect of the new church was Edward Lapidge, who had earlier designed St Peter's, Hammersmith.[4] He provided a typical large town church, with galleries and box pews, capable of seating 800 people. In 1973 this church in turn was largely destroyed by fire. It was rebuilt within the old walls on a more open plan, with fewer seats, no galleries and the seats facing north rather than east.

THE FIRST NONCONFORMISTS

The Church of England was virtually unchallenged at Putney until the late eighteenth century, except by the few Quakers during Charles II's reign. In 1788 the minister could claim that there were no nonconformists or 'papists' whatever. In this, Putney differed from neighbours such as Wandsworth and Mortlake, probably because it was dominated by the respectable in their great houses and because of the absence

169. The Platt Mission, c.1960.

of an independent-minded industrial workforce. Not that everyone attended St Mary's however: in 1758, 'the church is duly frequented on the Lord's day but not so much by the poor as I could wish'; and in 1788, 'too many absent themselves from the church'.[5]

In 1799 a room in Felsham Road near Gay Street was licensed for meetings of an independent congregation, under the auspices of the Surrey Mission Society. The minister of Putney denounced it in 1807 as follows (wrongly describing it as Methodist):

> There is a licensed room for a class of Methodists, who are trained up in error by the ministers of the Itinerant Society. There are not more than four householders in the parish who contribute to the support of this room; but the expenses are defrayed by frequent collections from those whom curiosity or dissipation leads there. At present the number of regular attendants is very inconsiderable, but should they be enabled as they threaten to build a chapel, there is great reason to fear that the want of accommodation in the parish church would drive many of the lower classes to resort to these seducing teachers.[6]

His fears were realised. In 1808 they opened a purpose-built chapel in the Platt, and it was clearly popular, being enlarged in 1827 and 1830. Its baptism register of 1827-34 suggests that the majority of its members were working people from nearby streets, such as gardeners, painters and shoemakers. The congregation moved to a new church in Oxford Road in 1872, later amalgamating with the Union Church, but the old chapel continued to be used as a mission hall.[7] In the 1960s the old chapel was demolished and a new one built in Felsham Road. It is now one of the Shaftesbury Society's Christian Mission Centres.

VICTORIAN AND EDWARDIAN GROWTH

The Church of England acquired three additional churches at Putney in the Victorian and Edwardian period, and Putney at last became a separate parish in about 1860 (at first part of the Diocese of London, then Rochester in 1877 and Southwark in 1905).[8] St John's was consecrated in 1859 as a chapel of ease. It was built largely at the expense of John Temple Leader, who had a home on Putney Hill and was developing much of the nearby area. The architect was Charles Lee, who had been a pupil of John Nash, and many of whose buildings, including St John's, give the impression of being older than they are. St John's was enlarged in 1888.[9] After the fire at St Mary's it served as the parish church, but in 1977 it was declared redundant and sold to the Polish Roman Catholics.

All Saints on the Lower Common was consecrated in 1874. The site was former common land which had been given by Earl Spencer. The architect was G.E. Street, who also designed the Law Courts in the Strand. It has a rich and colourful interior, with a painted roof and fine stained-glass windows executed from designs by Burne-Jones. The worshippers were expected to be largely working-class, so the church was to be supported by collections at services rather than by the usual means of pew rents.[10]

170. St John's Church, c.1890.

A third chapel of ease to St Mary's – St Margaret's – had a more chequered career. It was originally a Baptist chapel, which Colonel Alexander Croll of Granard Lodge built in Putney Park Lane in about 1859 as a memorial to his mother. The chapel door

171. St Margaret's Church as it originally appeared, entered by a flight of steps, before it became an Anglican church.

was approached by a flight of steps, and inside the floor was raked like a theatre. In 1879 Croll transferred the chapel to the Presbyterians, who used it for nearly twenty years. After that it faced an uncertain future; one plan was to turn it into a laundry. It was eventually given by Seth Taylor, then owner of Granard Lodge, to the Church of England. The outside steps were removed and the floor levelled, and under the name of St Margaret's (as requested by Seth Taylor), it was reopened in 1912. In 1923, as the Dover House Estate neared completion, St Margaret's became a separate parish.[11]

The number of Nonconformist churches grew even more impressively, reaching ten by 1903. In 1843 Methodist services were being held over a carpenter's shop near Walker's Place, and two years later a small chapel, known as the Hole in the Wall, was built at the corner of Stratford Grove and Lacy Road (where Ferry House now stands). In 1870 it was replaced by a new Methodist Chapel on the present site in the Upper Richmond Road. The present church was added in 1882, and a large hall in 1907. We may sometimes wonder why the Victorians built such large churches, particularly the Putney Methodists, with a membership of only 62 in 1882, but in this case we know the reason: a wealthy Methodist had donated £10,000 to build ten new churches on condition that each could seat at least a thousand people, and Putney qualified for a share of this. The church suffered in its early days from the involvement of its minister, George Dyson, in the Adelaide Bartlett poison trial (1886), in which he was a co-defendant with a married woman on a charge of murdering her husband. In 1902 the Putney Methodists were said to be 'nearly all country-born people who, having acquired the habit of chapel-going in the country, continue it here'.[12]

In 1857 a breakaway group from the Platt, seeking a completely non-denominational fellowship, formed what became the Union Church in the Upper Richmond Road and appealed to members of all the denominations to join them. The foundation stone was laid in 1861. It was usually described as Congregational and Baptist. Services continued in the Union Church until about 1960, and it now forms Group 64's Goodrich Theatre.[13]

Other churches included the Baptist Church in Werter Road (established there in 1876, the present building dating from 1884); Emmanuel Church in the Upper Richmond Road, near the corner of Oxford Road (1881); Sefton Street Mission (c.1892, but subsequently rebuilt); and the Presbyterian Church (now United Reformed) in Briar Walk (1897). Emmanuel Church belonged to the Free Church of England, 'a body with very strong anti-Ritualistic and anti-Popery views'. It remained in use until the Second World

172. *Emmanuel Church, Upper Richmond Road, c.1907.*

War, and was finally demolished in the 1970s.[14]

The Roman Catholics had no church in Putney until 1900, when a temporary site was obtained occupying part of what is now the gardens of 28 to 32 Hazlewell Road.[15] The 'iron church' built there is believed to be still in use on a different site as 32A Hazlewell Road. In 1903 Lady Westbury gave land in Hazlewell Road for the Church of St Simon Stock, and the building of the present church began three years later.

Both in Putney and elsewhere in London the clergy were very disappointed with the numbers who attended their new churches. Putney's Presbyterian minister observed in 1902 that 'the middle class here are as indifferent to religious observances as the poor elsewhere'. According to Charles Booth, 'there is perhaps no spot in London where religion plays a more unsatisfactory part than it does in Putney, and the lack of Christian unity appears to be exceptionally marked', at least between Anglicans and nonconformists: 'It may seem incredible that men ... seeking to serve the same Master, should pass and re-pass in the streets for a quarter of a century and never speak'.[16]

Booth may have overdone the gloom, which partly reflected the high ambitions of the Victorian clergy. A census of church attendance in London in 1902-3 recorded 4974 people attending services on the relevant Sunday in Putney and Roehampton: 2,388 at the four Anglican churches, 620 Methodists, 552 at the Union Church's two buildings, 465 Baptists, 264 Presbyterians, 409 at four other Nonconformist churches, and 276 Catholics. Taking into account people who attended twice (reckoned to be 39%), and the census organisers' estimate that about half the population was too young, too old, too busy or too sick to attend, just over a third of those who could have attended church did so - a slightly higher proportion than in the London County Council area as a whole (1 in 2.7).[17]

ROEHAMPTON

The early ecclesiastical history of Roehampton is an odd one. The first place of worship there was a chapel attached to Sir Richard Weston's Great House, consecrated in 1632. It was licensed for use only by the inhabitants of Weston's house; everyone else was supposed to go to Putney Church. By 1758, however, the chapel was being used more widely, much to the distress of Putney's minister, who lost the gratuities from a prosperous area while still having to carry out the parochial duties in 'that distant part of the parish'. In 1777 the old chapel was replaced by a new one adjoining Roehampton Lane. This was very much a commercial venture, built without any ecclesiastical authority, and was never even consecrated. It was leased for £25 a year to a clergyman, who presumably made a living from it by means of pew rents.

As Roehampton's population increased, it was decided to rebuild the chapel, and a new one on the same site was consecrated in 1843 amid great rejoicing: 'By a subscription among the gentry, tickets for meat, bread, beer, etc., were distributed among the poorer families of the hamlet, that all might participate in the festive observance of the day'. For the first time Roehampton had a church intended for all its inhabitants rather than just the rich. Roehampton became a chapelry district in 1845 and a parish in 1862.[18]

Despite several enlargements this church too had to be replaced by a larger one, and a new site was found on the edge of the Common. The new church, designed by G.H. Fellows Prynne, was consecrated in 1898. It is certainly large and well-equipped, for more money was subscribed than was actually needed. Important features are the 200 foot spire and the traceried stone screen filling the whole of the chancel arch, inspired by the medieval screen at Great Bardfield in Essex.[19] The altar in the the Lady Chapel is believed to have been used in all four buildings.

The second place of worship in Roehampton was not a church at all but a synagogue, built at the back

173. The second Roehampton Chapel, of 1777.

174. The third Roehampton Chapel, consecrated in 1843.

175. Laying the foundation stone of the present Holy Trinity Church, Roehampton, 1896.

of Elm Grove when it was occupied by Benjamin Goldsmid, a greatly respected Jewish financier (known as 'the Benevolent Jew'). It probably disappeared after his suicide in 1808.[20]

There has been a Catholic presence at Roehampton since the mid-19th century. Elm Grove was bought by the Society of the Sacred Heart in 1850 and the present convent was established. The Digby Stuart Training College, named after two of its superiors, Mothers Digby and Stuart, now shares the site with the convent. In 1861 the Jesuits bought Parksted as a noviciate (or training college), renaming it Manresa House after an incident in the life of their founder; they retained it until 1962. The best-known of the novices at Manresa House was the poet, Gerard Manley Hopkins (1844-89), and there are many references to Roehampton in his diaries. Nearby was the noviciate of the Poor Servants of the Mother of God, who in 1876 obtained their present site, St Mary's Convent in Roehampton High Street, where they care for about a hundred handicapped girls. The Jesuits assumed responsibility for parish work at Roehampton, and in 1881 St Joseph's Church was consecrated.[21]

Also at Roehampton from at least 1889 to 1914 was a Nonconformist mission hall at 2 Medfield Street. There had been some local hostility to the Jesuits when they arrived in 1861, but Booth wrote in 1902 that in Roehampton 'all sects pull together under the leadership of the Church of England, affording, in this respect, a contrast to the neighbouring parish of Putney. Very friendly relations prevail in this pleasant little community'.[22]

RECENT TIMES

The story of religion in Putney and Roehampton since the early twentieth century is similar to that elsewhere: declining congregations, churches closed, friendlier relations between Christian denominations, and the appearance of new Christian sects and other religions. Of the 14 churches in 1918 (excluding the various mission halls) two have closed (the Union Church and Emmanuel Church) and one has been transferred to a body new to the area (the Polish Roman Catholics). The building of the post-war council estates gave rise to just one new church. The Methodists on the Alton Estate at first held services in a school, until in 1967 they were able to build a Christian Community Centre, where the minister works in conjunction with the Anglicans as part of an 'ecumenical parish'.

A new church built at the back of the former Union Church in 1968 currently houses the Liberal Catholic Church. The Christian (or Plymouth) Brethren built a hall in Norroy Road. The Sixth Church of Christ Scientist (Christian Scientists) was established in Chelverton Road by 1914, and between the wars erected its present building in the Upper Richmond Road. In the 1930s there was a small Spiritualist Church at 309 Upper Richmond Road. There is a Jewish synagogue in Chelverton Road. There may be fewer attenders than at the start of the present century, but there are probably more places of worship in Putney and Roehampton now than ever before.[23]

Educating Putney

THE WATERMEN'S SCHOOL

The sons of watermen benefited from the parish's first charity school. Under the will of Thomas Martyn, a wealthy resident who died in 1684, a school for 20 sons of Putney watermen was to be established and endowed with his substantial estates, provided that his niece (and heiress) died childless, as she shortly afterwards did. According to tradition, Martyn had once been saved from drowning by a waterman, but it is just as likely that he viewed the watermen and their sons as poor men deserving assistance. 'A fair and large house' was to be built, and 'the Mathematticks' was to be taught. (In fact reading and writing were taught too). The scholars were to receive their board and lodging, together with one grey coat lined with red and other clothing each year.[1]

After protracted legal wrangling, a fine schoolhouse was constructed on the south side of Putney Bridge Road and the school eventually opened in 1718. It performed an immensely useful service for two centuries, and seems to have been appreciated by the watermen: in the 1820s, when it came under threat, they declared themselves 'confident that the liberal education that their sons received in Martyn's surpassed the education of the national system of learning'. In 1911 the school was closed by the London County Council, which considered it too small, but the charity continues as an educational trust, making grants to the sons and daughters of watermen.[2]

Apart from charity schools, there is often little surviving evidence of schools for the less prosperous. Some may well have existed at Putney, since even tradesmen and craftsmen needed to be able to write bills, and in 1679 Henry Burman, a cooper, was proceeded against for undertaking to teach boys without having a licence to do so.[3] For the poor, however, educational provision was intermittent (at best) right up to the late eighteenth century. In 1717 and 1718, A. Char was paid by the churchwardens 'for schooling for parish children', but in 1719 there is only an entry 'for a year's schooling of Shuter's child', and thereafter nothing.[4] However, a school supported by subscriptions from parishioners could well have existed without leaving any trace in the parish records. From 1751, no boy was to be admitted to the watermen's school unless he already knew his letters, which supports this idea, and the will of John Price, dated

176. The Watermen's School, opened in 1718. The building was demolished to make way for the District Railway, after which the school moved to smaller premises.

177. A boy of the Watermen's School, 1826 (watercolour by Hassell).

1772, describes him as 'parish clerk and schoolmaster'.[5] Nevertheless, in 1788 there was said to be no voluntary charity school, and the parish schools set up in 1789 were regarded as a new venture.[6]

PUTNEY'S EDUCATIONAL REVOLUTION

Education for the poor in Putney was transformed in the three decades after 1789. This was achieved by the parish schools (sometimes called National Schools). They were founded as Sunday schools in 1789, and two years later became day schools for 20 boys and 20 girls.[7] They soon began to expand, so that in 1819 the parish could claim that 'All the children of the poor have the means of education in the national schools' - a striking change from the situation several decades earlier.[8] They were described as follows in 1807:

> There are two schools supported by voluntary contributions, in one of which forty boys from the age of seven to twelve are taught to read and write; and in the other twenty-five girls from the age of eight to fourteen are taught reading and needle work: their clothing and a dinner which is given them every Sunday are defrayed partly out of the profits arising from the girls' labours. The religious principles in which they are instructed are those of the Established Church, in which they are frequently examined by the parochial minister as well as by other benefactors.[9]

This was the period when the Church of England at last woke up to the need to provide schools for the

178. Putney's National Schools, 1826 (watercolour by Hassell).

179. A class at Roehampton Church School in about 1903.

poor. The aims were to provide religious knowledge, to impart certain attitudes considered desirable (such as obedience), and to root out idleness, as well as to teach some elementary reading and writing. These mixed motives are reflected at Putney, where, as indicated above, the girls' school was run as a 'School of Industry'. An attempt was made in 1800 to do the same with the boys' school; a Mr Churchland was to teach the boys 'weaving, carpeting and other manufacturing for sale', receiving in return £40 a year and 5% of any profits, but this plan foundered after five years.[10] Another attempt was made in 1829: in addition to the needlework already done by the girls, 'the girls have been instructed in knitting stockings, &c. &c.; and the boys in making garden nets, &c., which has proved a useful employment for them, without any detriment to their usual instruction in the rudiments of religion, reading, and writing'. However, the profits from this work were insignificant. Fees were charged in the parish schools from 1829 until 1905, but the schools' income came mainly from subscriptions and collections in church.[11] In 1829 it was stated that children were allowed to remain at the schools until the age of 14, 'unless they can obtain employment sooner'.

At first the children may have been taught in the church, but in 1819 the site in Felsham Road still occupied by St Mary's Parochial School was obtained. (The present building there dates from 1867). The number of pupils rose gradually to 276 in 1849, by which time the parish schools provided two-thirds of all the school places for children under 13 in Putney. Even so, it was difficult to keep pace with the growing population. A survey made in 1849 revealed that over 350 children aged up to 13 who were capable of attending school were unprovided for. The parish responded by establishing a school for 250 infants in 1852, and a school for 100 on the Lower Common in 1857. The latter was to be called 'the Penny School' (or All Saints School), and was intended for 'the indigent poor of Putney'.[12]

At Roehampton, Lady Bessborough of Manresa House started a school for some of the village's poor children in 1798, but what we know as Roehampton Church School began in 1828 as an infant school for 20 children. It acquired premises on former common land in 1836 (now the junior school, by Roehampton Lane). A site for a boys' school was obtained in 1854 and its original classroom survives.[13] The boys' and girls' schools remained separate until 1945.

180. Putney Upper Grade Church of England School in Walkers Place, 1923. The building is now let for commercial use.

The proportion of brides and grooms who could sign their names in the marriage register (as opposed to putting a mark) indicates the impact of the parish schools. In the late eighteenth century in Putney about 60% of men and 40% of women signed. These proportions rapidly rose after about 1800, until in the 1850s about 80% of both men and women signed their names.[14]

VICTORIAN SCHOOLS AND COLLEGES

The parish schools and watermen's school continued to be supplemented by private schools. In 1871 there were four private day schools, such as that of George Newboult, aged 47, in Walkers Place, where he had been teaching for 26 years. Newboult was then teaching 21 boys, most aged between 5 and 13, for 4 to 5 hours a day, 5 days a week, and 48 weeks a year; all were taught reading, and some were taught writing, arithmetic, dictation, RI, grammar and 'words and meanings and spelling'. The government inspector considered both the teaching and the premises satisfactory. At the other extreme in 1871 was Miss Mariana Williams, aged 17 (and already a teacher for three years) at 15 Gay Street. In a room 12 feet square she was teaching 30 children aged up to 6 for 51 weeks a year at fees of 2d. to 6d. a week. The inspector damned it as 'a cottage room without furniture or apparatus, crammed full of children'.[15]

Ever since the seventeenth century Putney had had schools for children of the well-to-do from a wider area, such as that of Mrs Bregantz, a French woman, in Cromwell House, Putney Bridge Road, where two sisters of Mary Wollstonecraft, author of *Vindication of the rights of woman* (1792) were teachers in 1790.[16] In 1851 there were four boarding schools, ranging from Emma Thompson's in the High Street, with seven pupils aged from 10 to 16, to the Revd William Carmalt's, which occupied Putney House on the site of Carmalt Gardens. This lasted from 1802 to the 1850s and catered for 'young men principally designed for the public schools and the learned professions'.[17] The 1851 census recorded Carmalt's successor (the Revd Edward Trimmer), four assistant masters (two for Classics, one mathematics and one French), 44 resident pupils aged from 7 to 16, and 11 servants.

A more unusual establishment was the Putney College for Civil Engineers, occupying two large houses by the river in the Deodar Road area. It was founded in 1839 and achieved a high reputation during its 18 years of existence. The 1851 census records the Principal and his family, three assistant masters, 37 students and 20 servants. The students, aged from 16 to 24, came from all over the world, including India, the USA, Italy, the West Indies and Ireland.

181. The Revd Carmalt's School, in Putney House, Upper Richmond Road, in the early nineteenth century.

The importance of this institution lay in giving practical tuition in applied science at a time when the universities were still dominated by the Classics. A prospectus of 1848 clearly shows the College's prestige: the President and Vice Presidents comprised three dukes, a marquess, four earls, three other lords, a baronet, a major-general and a professor. The prospectus boasted that 'The object of this institution is to provide a liberal, practical education, on a scale not hitherto attainable in this country. To the ordinary routine of study necessary for a gentleman, is added special instruction in the PRACTICAL application of scientific principles. Though at first intended for the professions of civil engineer and architect, it has been found that the system holds out advantages for many other professions and pursuits'. The College closed in 1857.[18]

In 1876 the parish widened the scope of its schools by establishing one for the children of small tradespeople and artisans on the Lower Common (replacing the 'Penny School'). 'This class', it was said, 'probably more than any other, influences the opinion of the still lower classes, and it would be great benefit to both classes, if the former had the means of obtaining within the Parish, a sound education fitted for their requirements, and under the influence of the Church'.[19] (The present All Saints School dates from 1893-6.)

By that time the parish was facing the threat of secular competition. The great Education Act of 1870 reflected the new idealism which saw education as the right of every child, as well as the need to educate classes which had recently acquired the vote. Local boards were to be set up to establish schools if existing local provision was inadequate. Attendance at school finally became compulsory in 1880. Putney Parish was anxious to avert 'the mischief' of a board school, which would entice children away from its own schools,[20] but the mischief duly arrived in 1900 at 13 Deodar Road. It moved nine years later to a purpose-built school in Hotham Road, which it still occupies. Just over the parish boundary another board school called Brandlehow opened in 1902.

THE TWENTIETH CENTURY

A third board school, Huntingfield, opened in 1922 to serve the newly-built Dover House Estate. The first Catholic school in Putney (apart from a brief venture serving the Irish of Biggs Row in the 1880s) was Our Lady of Victories in Clarendon Drive, founded in 1925.

Change since the Second World War has been more rapid. New primary schools included Ibstock Place (the 'demonstration school' for Froebel, transferred from Kensington in 1946), Granard (1953), Heathmere (1954), Beavers' Holt (1956), Danebury (1958), and Roehampton Gate (1959). Also new to the area were Chartfield (1960) and Greenmead (1964), at first for delicate and physically handicapped children respectively.

In the nineteenth and early twentieth centuries, children might spend their whole school life in one school, though the parish established a separate Upper Grade Girls' School in Walker's Place and an Upper Grade Boys' School at All Saints. The gradual raising of the school leaving age and the reorganisation of secondary education gave rise to two comprehensive schools serving Putney and the surrounding area. The Elliott School moved from Merton Road to Putney in 1956 to become a comprehensive for 2000 children - the LCC's first co-educational comprehensive. Just outside the parish was Mayfield School, first established in 1907, which became a comprehensive in 1956. The transfer of responsibility for education to Wandsworth Borough Council and its decision to re-establish selection are likely to result in further changes. In recent years declining numbers of pupils have resulted in school closures, including Mayfield in 1984 and Huntingfield in 1993.

Local further education institutions included two teacher training colleges: Froebel (1921) and Digby Stuart (founded in 1875 and moved to Roehampton in 1946). In 1975 these joined with Whitelands in West Hill and Southlands in Parkside to form Roehampton Institute of Higher Education, with 3000 students and 300 teaching staff. It is now intended to combine them on the Froebel/Digby Stuart site. In the early 1960s, Mount Clare and Downshire House were taken over by Garnett College as a training college for technical teachers, and they now form part of the University of Greenwich. The Putney College of Education on Putney Hill opened in 1969 for 200 full-time day students, 800 students attending courses run in conjunction with industry and 2,000 evening students; it is now the Putney Building of South Thames College. The Putney School of Art in Oxford Road was founded in 1895.

As for private schools, many failed to survive the war and evacuation, and the longest-established (Willington School in Colinette Road, founded in 1885) moved to Wimbledon in 1991, but the survivors and newcomers include Glengyle (1907) in Carlton Drive, Hurlingham (1947) in Deodar Road, and Putney Park (1953) in Woodborough Road. The best known is Putney High School, under the control of the Girls' Public Day School Trust. It opened in 1893 in a house on the corner of Oakhill Road and the Upper Richmond Road (now replaced by Oakhill Court). Between 1910 and 1915 it moved to its present site on Putney Hill. There it continues a tradition going back to the time of Samuel Pepys and John Evelyn.

182. The College for Civil Engineers, in Putney House by the Thames, 1843. (The College also occupied the Cedars next door.)

Modern Putney

BETWEEN THE WARS

By far the largest development between the wars was the LCC's Roehampton Estate (now the Dover House Estate), occupying the western half of the former Putney Park. The site, purchased in 1919, stretched all the way from the Upper Richmond Road to Putney Heath, and consisted chiefly of two mansions (Dover House and Putney Park House) and their grounds. The land south of Crestway was leased for private development, while the LCC developed the area to the north in 1920-7 as a 'cottage estate' with 1,212 houses, accommodating about 4,400 people.[1] For Putney this was development on an unprecedented scale. Many of the existing features of the site were retained, including Putney Park House, Putney Park Lane, the Footpath and numerous trees. Land was provided for tennis courts, allotments and a school. The development derived largely from pre-war garden city ideals, and was widely (and rightly) acclaimed.

Wandsworth Borough Council's one development was the Henry Jackson Estate - 88 flats in Felsham Road replacing the slums of Biggs Row and neighbouring alleys in 1936-7. Private developments included the southern part of the Dover House site (from 1924), much of Chartfield and Westleigh Avenues, the grounds of Templeton (Roehampton Gate and Roedean Crescent, laid out in 1932) and Bowling Green Close (1933).[2] Otherwise the private sector built flats, especially in the mid-1930s. Some of these were spacious and of architectural distinction, especially Manor Fields (1933), with 220 flats, and Fairacres in Roehampton Lane (1937). Other examples are Roehampton Close (1933), Wellwood Court (1938), Harwood Court, Belvedere Court, Ormonde Court (1935), Balmuir Court (1940), Lower Park (1934), King's Keep (1936), Ullswater, Heath Rise (1935), Exeter House (1935), Highlands Heath, Wildcroft (1936) and Ross Court.[3] In total, these 16 developments provided 1102 flats housing about 4,000 people. Similar developments would probably have continued but for the war.

INDUSTRIES AND OFFICES

Putney never became wholly a dormitory suburb. There has been a significant range of industries, mostly small-scale and short-lived, of which only a few can be mentioned here. Putney's long association with brewing continued until the 1960s, when what had been the Anchor Brewery was closed, though in its latter years it was only a bottling plant. A map of 1907 shows not only the former Anchor Brewery and the long-established Dallett's soap factory, but also a candle and night-light factory north of Felsham Road, a scientific instruments factory in Premier Place, J. Dean's flag, blind and tent factory at the back of Russell's Yard (off the High Street), a van builder north of Dallett's soap factory, William Douglas & Sons' refrigerating machinery factory at Douglas Wharf, and A.G. Douglas & Brothers' athletics goods factory at Putney Wharf.[4] Dean's Blinds later moved to a site by the river, and more recently to Earlsfield. At Roehampton is the artificial limb-making factory,

183. Building work on the Dover House Estate in about 1921.

184. *Douglas Wharf, Brewhouse Lane.*

185. *The planned layout of Manor Fields, 1933.*

186. Making munitions boxes in Adamson's premises (now replaced by Sainsbury's supermarket) during the First World War.

187. The former Baldfaced Stag on the right and the first part of the new KLG factory on the left, 1937.

188. Advertisement by Palladium Autocars in 1924. The company was founded in West Kensington in 1911, moved to the former horse bus depot at 38 Felsham Road, Putney, in 1914, and remained in business there until 1925.

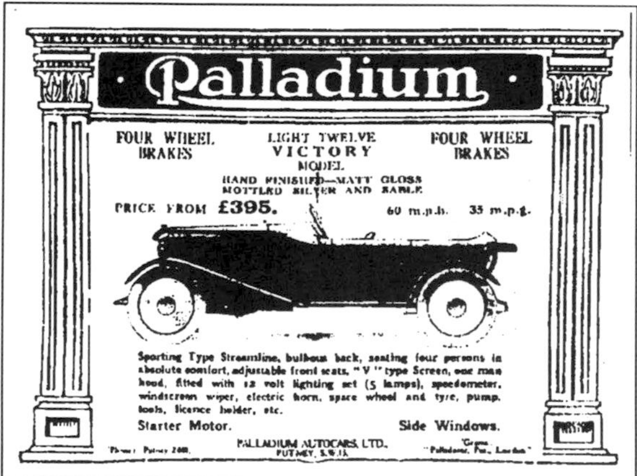

which came into existence with Queen Mary's Hospital in 1915. There were a number of automobile manufacturers, such as Palladium Autocars at 38 Felsham Road from 1914 to 1925 and others in Premier Place.[5]

The most important enterprise established in the parish was the KLG works in Putney Vale. Kenelm Lee Guinness, an enthusiastic racing car driver, designed a new type of spark plug for car and aircraft engines, capable of withstanding intense heat, in the cellars of the former Baldfaced Stag in 1912. It was an immediate success, and production increased quickly, especially during the First World War: by 1918 KLG was employing over 1,200 people, making it probably the largest ever employer in Putney and Roehampton. It was taken over in 1927 by Smiths Industries, which built a new factory there in 1937-9. This was demolished in 1989,

189. Slum clearance in the Platt, c.1960.

but Smiths Industries still has a factory on an adjacent site, where one of the products is jet engine igniters, the modern equivalent of the spark plug.[6]

Large-scale office accommodation appeared in Putney after the Second World War, with office blocks being built between East Putney Station and Putney Hill and around St Mary's Church.

POST-WAR DEVELOPMENT

The themes since the Second World War have been the making good of bomb damage, a small amount of slum clearance, the building of council estates on the grounds of the remaining great houses, and the more efficient use of existing housing land through re-building or subdivision. Between 1940 and 1945 Putney and Roehampton experienced 1000 bombing incidents, in which 399 people were killed, 1,377 were injured and numerous buildings were destroyed or damaged. Some destroyed buildings were replaced by prefabricated dwellings ('pre-fabs'), which were intended to have a short life but are in some cases still there (for example in St John's Avenue).

The most important changes were the large LCC estates, especially the Alton and Ashburton Estates. The latter took the sites of Ripon House, Grantham House, Ashburton House, Ashburton Cottage and Gifford House beside Putney Heath, as well as an area further north bounded by Chartfield, Gwendolen and Westleigh Avenues. (The ice-house belonging to Gifford House survives at the top of Putney Park Lane.) In their place from 1951 arose a spacious layout of two-storey houses and five-storey flats. With its plentiful open space and generally low-rise housing it was still largely in the tradition of the cottage estates.

The Alton Estates were even larger. They were planned to house just under 100 people per acre, double the density on the Dover House Estate. The Alton East Estate was built first (1952-5), occupying the sites of the Victorian mansions of Roehampton Park. The later Alton West Estate (1955-9) provided a testing ground for the policy of building tall blocks of flats. It occupied the grounds of Manresa House, Downshire House and Mount Clare. Point blocks were built of up to 12 storeys, and high slab blocks containing up to 75 flats each, with the result that large areas such as Downshire Field could be left as open space. If high-rise estates were ever to be successful they would be successful here, with plenty of space and Richmond Park on the doorstep, and the Alton West Estate certainly has its defenders, but the policy of building tall blocks of flats has since been discredited.

The two Alton Estates housed about 9,500 people,

190. *The Alton West Estate, looking towards Roehampton village.*

chiefly from homes being cleared in Battersea and White City, and they transformed Roehampton, for which the 1950s were comparable to the 1880s in Putney. In 1981, 90% of Roehampton's households occupied council housing, compared with 31% in Greater London as a whole.[7]

The last of the major LCC/GLC estates was built in about 1970 on the grounds of the Priory Nursing Home, displacing the parish's last herd of cows. Meanwhile, Wandsworth Borough Council had been pursuing a housing programme of its own, though it usually had to be content with smaller sites. These were often compulsorily purchased (in the case of large houses) or were slums or bomb sites. Examples of the replacement of slums were Crown Court in the Quill/Lacy Road triangle in the early 1960s, and Gay Street, the first part of which, including the ten-storey Phelps House, was completed in 1965.[8] The Council's one large development was the isolated Putney Vale Estate, where it was able to use surplus cemetery land. It also took over the site of the Priory Lane Swimming Pools, which became the Woking Estate.

Private house-building was slow to begin after the war, with most of the resources used in the public sector and licenses being required. Granard Avenue, most of which dates from the early 1950s, was one of the few substantial private developments. Demolition of large houses got under way in the 1960s, especially once the 99-year leases on the Lime Grove Estate began to fall in in 1965. Most of the Cambalt Road houses disappeared in the 1970s. They were generally replaced by blocks of flats, though sometimes by terraced houses. Many large houses were subdivided.

But for the Leasehold Reform Act of 1967, which gave leaseholders the right to buy the freehold of their property, Putney might well have changed significantly in the 1970s and 1980s, as the 99-year leases made in the 1870s and 1880s fell in. As it is, only the houses where Booth's classification was 'wealthy' or, at the other end of the scale, 'poverty and comfort (mixed)' or 'moderate poverty' have succumbed in any number. Most recent developments have been small-scale, often involving building on the ends of gardens, a process reminiscent of seventeenth century Putney. Victorian and Edwardian Putney of the well-to-do and comfortable classes remains largely intact, and in much of Putney one has only to imagine the scene without cars and mature trees to see it as the first inhabitants of those streets did.

Putney has acquired a number of prominent non-residential buildings since the war. Among the least satisfactory have been the office buildings, especially the ICL building by St Mary's Church, one of Putney's relatively few eyesores. The 1980s, characteristically, has provided retail emporia: the Asda supermarket in

191. Putney Exchange, 1990.

Putney Vale (1989) and Putney Exchange in Putney High Street (opened in 1990). The most satisfactory building of recent decades is the Putney Leisure Centre in the Upper Richmond Road (designed by Powell and Moya and opened in 1968), to which can perhaps be added the restored St Mary's Church.

Physical change has been accompanied by major social and political changes, especially in Roehampton. The parliamentary seat of Putney (somewhat larger than the old parish) changed hands in 1964 - from Conservative to Labour – for the first time since its creation in 1918. More recently, change has been in the other direction, symbolised by the Conservatives regaining the Parliamentary seat in 1979. Large houses have ceased to be subdivided (partly as a deliberate result of planning policies), some streets have been 'gentrified', and council houses have been sold to their tenants. This has in turn brought about physical changes, notably on the Dover House Estate, where new owners have remodelled their houses.

Another important aspect of post-war Putney is the Putney Society, founded in 1959, initially to defend a threatened tree in Crestway. The tree survived, and the Society now has 1200 members and a significant influence on local planning policies. As in 1864-71, when the Commons were saved, it is the commitment of local people to the safeguarding and improvement of their environment which is the best security that Putney will remain an attractive place to live.

192. The ICL building (behind St Mary's) under construction in the mid 1950s.

Notes

Abbreviations

Booth	Charles Booth, *The life and labours of the people in London*, part 3 (1902).
CRW 1 and 3	*Extracts from the court rolls of the manor of Wimbledon, 1461-1864* (1866-8), vols. 1-2 and 3 respectively.
CWA 1 and 2	Putney churchwardens' accounts, 1623-92 and 1693-1771 (Greater London Record Office, P95/MRY1/413 and 414).
Donelan	C.M. Donelan, *Putney Town and Putney Parish*, unpublished manuscript in Wandsworth Museum.
HLRO	House of Lords Record Office, private bill evidence
LPL	Lambeth Palace Library
NRO	Northamptonshire Record Office
PRO	Public Record Office
SC	Sale catalogues (in author's possession unless indicated otherwise)
SRO	Surrey Record Office
WBN	*Wandsworth Borough News*
WH	*Wandsworth Historian* (published by Wandsworth Historical Society).
WLHC	Borough of Wandsworth, Local History Collection, Battersea Library.
WHNS	Wandsworth Historical Society News-Sheet.
WP	Wandsworth Papers (published by Wandsworth Historical Society; Nos. 8 and 9 are forthcoming).

Notes

Settlers, Centurions and Peasants and *A Changing Landscape* are chiefly based on WHS, *Early Putney*, WP 9, and *A Place in the Country* and *A Prosperous Community* chiefly on WH 43 (1984), 15-22, and WH 49 (1986), 1-7, where fuller references can be found. See also WH forthcoming on Roman Putney.

Introduction

1. John Blair, *Early medieval Surrey* (1991), 39-40.
2. Below, p.
3. Except briefly in the 1650s.
4. SRO, 369/4, 14 July 1685.
5. WH 60 (1990), 1.

Settlers, Centurions and Peasants

1. PRO, C11/853/122.
2 London and Middlesex Archaeological Society, *Transactions*, XXIX (1978), 54.
3. For this section, see WH 48 (1986), 1-5; WH 50 (1986), 1-8; WH 52 (1987), 15-21; WP9.
4. Peter Marsden, *Roman London* (1980), chaps. I & II,
5. WH 52 (1987), 9.
6. WH 13 (1975), 1-7; WH 57 (1989), 9-12.
7. Charles Hailstone, *Alleys of Mortlake and East Sheen* (1983), 8.
8. N. Fuentes, *Land division in Roman London* (unpublished dissertation, Institute of Archaeology, London, 1985), 37-48.
9 See e.g. Trevor Rowley, *Villages in the landscape* (1978), chap. 4.
10. Alan Vince, *Saxon London* (1990), 6-8, 130, 150-1.
11. J.E.B. Gover *et al*, *The place-names of Surrey* (English Place-Name Society XI, 1934), 27; London Record Society XII (1976), 28; WH 36 (1983), 7.
12. WH 57 (1989), 12, 14.
13. WH 15 (1977), 5-8.
14. WH 36 (1983), 10; Gover *et al*, 28; WH 39 (1983), 4; CWA1, ff. 3-4.
15. WH 14 (1976), 5; WH 23 (1979), 1-4; WH 39 (1983), 5-7.
16. WH 31 (1981), 7-10.
17 WH 36 (1983), 8-9.
18. WH 36 (1983), 9.
19. WHNS No. 91 (1970).

A Changing Landscape

1. WH 51 (1986), 1-8; WH 52 (1987), 8-13; WH 53 (1987), 7-9.
2 D. Gerhold, *A map of Roehampton in 1617*, WP8.
3. *Ibid.*
4. WH 25 (1979), 1-4.
5. WH 14 (1976), 4.
6. Surrey Record Society No. 33 (1931). (Names modernised in text.)
7. NRO, SOX 136.
8. CRW3, 31; CRW1, 165.
9. NRO, SOX 136. Putney section transcribed in CRW 3, 166-92.
10. WHNS 1969/6.
11. J.G. Taylor, *Our Lady of Batersey* (1925), 304.
12. Gerhold, *Map of Roehampton*.
13. NRO, SOX 136.
14 CRW 1, 165.

A Place in the Country

1. F.M.L. Thompson, *Hampstead – building a borough 1650-1964* (1974), 8, 18-20.
2 Daniel Lysons, *The environs of London*, I (1792), 405.
3. R.B. Merriman, *Life and letters of Thomas Cromwell* (1902), 1-4.
4. *Ibid*, 8-9.
5. J.J. Scarisbrick, *Henry VIII* (1968), 383.
6. LPL, COMM V/5, 302.
7 Sir E.K. Chambers, *The Elizabethan stage* (1951) IV, 96-116.
8. PRO, PROB 5/1894; *Putney Society Review*, Spring 1978.
9. PRO, PROB 5/1892.
10. Daniel Defoe, *A tour through the whole island of Great Britain* (1971 Penguin edn), 177.

11. D. Gerhold, *Putney in 1636*, WP7 (1994), 10-11, 21-2.
12. Gerhold, *Map of Roehampton*.
13. *Surrey Archaeological Collections*, XXXVII (1927), 15, 26.
14. PRO, E112/248, No. 12.
15. NRO, SOX 182; WH 25 (1979), 4.

A Prosperous Community

1 At NRO; draft of the Putney section in British Library, Althorp Papers P 13.
2. Gerhold, *Putney in 1636*, 33.
3. PRO, E179/188/481.
4. WH 52 (1987), 12.
5. WLHC, Putney poor rate 1736.
6. WH 57 (1989), 18-20.
7. This section is based on the plotting of occupations (from parish registers, quarter sessions rolls etc.) against the 1664 hearth tax.
8. John Strype, *Survey of the Cities of London and Westminster* (1720).
9. PRO, C10/1/13; CWA 2, f.96; *Putney Society Review*, Spring 1979.
10. CWA 2, f.121.
11. E.G. Pine, *The Westminster Abbey singers* (1953).
12. See WH 65 (1992), 13-21.

Bridge and Town

1. PRO, PROB 5/1894; PRO, PROB 11/252, q.20.
2. *House of Commons Journals*, vol. 20 (1722-27), 597.
3. George and Michael Dewe, *Fulham Bridge 1729-1886* (1986).
4. William Albert, *The turnpike road system in England 1663-1840* (1972), 202-3; WH 17 (1977), 17.
5. Thomas De Laune, *The present state of London* (1681); Dewe, 79-80; J. Edwards, *Companion from London to Brighthelmston* (1801), 29-30; T.C. Barker & Michael Robbins, *A history of London Transport*, I, (1963), 21, 31, appendix 1.
6. Dewe, 119.
7. Dewe, 37.
8. *A charge on the parish: the treatment of poverty in Putney 1620-1834*, WP1 (1974).
9. NRO, SOX 496.
10. WLHC, Putney poor rate 1736; 1801 census.
11. WLHC, 1815 valuation (in Putney poor rate volume between 1807 and 1808).
12. NRO, SOX 496.
13. *Putney 1851*, WP 6 (1981), 15.
14. PRO, PROB 31/337/643.
15. WH 57 (1989), 18-20.

Villas and Mansions

1. Lysons, I, 433; A. Riches, 'Mount Clare, Roehampton', *Architectural History*, vol. 27 (1984), 256.
2 WLHC, Putney poor rates; Joan P. Alcock, *Where generations have trod* (1979), 60; Riches; SRO, 166/2a.
3. Guildhall Library, London, insertion in copy of Lysons; NRO, Spencer MS, Wimbledon copyhold cases, p.61; NRO, SOX 169, Putney Park.
4. Howard Colvin, *A biographical dictionary of British architects 1600-1840* (1978); Riches.
5. LPL, VP II/2/2b.
6. WH 34 (1982), 9-11.
7. Lysons, I, 62; WLHC, Putney poor rates; *The Metallurgicon local directory* (1867).
8. Guildhall Library, London, insertion in copy of Lysons.
9. WLHC, Putney poor rates 1736-94; SRO, land taxes 1780-1831; Greater London Record Office, P95/MRY1/57 to 89; directories. Dates are accurate to within a year.
10. WLHC, Putney poor rates.
11. See lists of churchwardens in CWA 1 & 2.
12. NRO, SOX 169, estate correspondence 1774-1887.
13. Gerhold, *Putney in 1636*, 28-9; British Library, Map Room, K. Top. XLI, 21d.
14. Alcock, 60.
15. British Library, Map Room, K. Top. XLI, 21d.
16. Alcock, 58; 1841 census.
17. Worcester Cathedral Library, tithe survey.
18. *Putney Society Review*, Spring 1978.
19. N. Pevsner, *London except the Cities of London and Westminster* (1952), 439.
20. Lady Charlotte Schreiber, *Extracts from her journal 1853-1891* (1952).
21. Donelan, 32-3.

A Modern Babylon

1. *Putney Society Review*, Spring 1978.
2. 1849 Putney tithe map (copy in SRO); *Putney – 1851*, WP 6 (1981), 4-5; Peter Gerhold, *The story of Coalecroft Road* (1977).
3 SC.
4. HLRO, Commons 1881 Vol. 29, 10 May.
5. WH 2 (1971), 12.
6. Booth, vol. 5, 212.
7. Booth, vol. 5, 219-20.
8. WLHC, SC.
9. Booth, vol. 5, 214, 219.
10. C. Furley Smith, *Twixt heath and river* (1908), 6, 69.
11. WH 2 (1971), 2-3.
12. WH 7 (1973), 1-5.
13. London Topographical Society *Newsletter*, 35 (1992), 3; *Putney – 1851*, 16; directories; WLHC, card index.
14. Donelan, 83, 140.
15. WBN, 25/1/1985, p.20.
16. WH 7 (1973), 7.
17. C. Furley-Smith, 65; Donelan, 136.
18. LCC, *Names of streets and places in the administrative County of London* (4th edn., 1955).
19. Booth, vol. 6, 97-8.

On the Move

1. NRO, SOX 496.
2. HLRO, Lords 1882 vol. 34, 25 July, p.7; Donelan, 144.
3. SRO, plans for City of London and Richmond Railway Bill 1836.

4. WLHC, Putney Vestry minutes 1842-53, p.90.
5. WH 42 (1984), 6; *Putney – 1851*, WP6 (1981), 24.
6. Tim Sherwood, *Change at Clapham Junction* (1994), 42-3; SC, Chelverton Road.
7. WH 8 (1973), 4-5.
8. WH 8 (1973), 5-6; WH 49 (1986), 8-13; WLHC, Putney Elected Vestry minutes, 8 Jan 1885.
9. WH 49 (1986), 13.
10. *Putney – 1851*, 26; [W.S. Clarke], *The suburban homes of London* (1881), 413; HLRO, Lords 1882 vol. 34, 25 July, 7.
11. Osbert Lancaster, *All done from memory* (1963), 52.
12. WHNS, 1960/6.

Open spaces

Unless indicated otherwise, the source for this chapter is Norman Plastow (ed.), *A history of Wimbledon & Putney Commons* (1986).

1. CRW 1; CRW 3.
2. CRW 1, 5, 9, 13, 19, 21, 25-7, 29, 38.
3. R.J. Milward, *Wimbledon at the time of the Civil War* (1976), 83.
4. C.J. Fèret, *Fulham old and new* (1900) I, 61-2.
5. W.A. Bartlett, *History and antiquities of Wimbledon* (1865), 189-92; Plastow.
6. Bartlett, 190-1.
7. CWA 2, p197.
8. CRW 1, 219; CWA 1, f.27.
9 CRW 1, *passim*.
10. NRO, SOX 36, Wimbledon 1788-1881, James Rice 1837.
11. WH 6 (1972), 3-6.
12. Lysons, 109; C.L. Collenette, *A history of Richmond Park* (1937), 5-6; PRO, C214/884.
13. CWA 1, ff.76, 95.
14. Michael Baxter Brown, *Richmond Park* (1985), 18-19, 73-4, 78, 115, 138.
15. Collenette, 51; letter from M.B. Brown to Peter Gerhold, 6 Sept 1982.

Rowing

1. HLRO, Commons 1872, vol. 43, 9 April, p.47.
2. A. Lloyd-Taylor, *Catalogue of the collection of rowing pictures and trophies at the Coach and Eight...Putney* (Whitbread & Co, c1954), 4-9.
3. Christopher Dodd, *The Oxford and Cambridge Boat Race* (1983), 63.
4. Eric Halladay, *Rowing in England: a social history – the amateur debate* (1990), 9-10, 25-6; WBN, 16/8/1963, p.7, 23/8/1963, p.5.
5 WBN, 21/10/1960.
6. Halladay, 57-9.
7. L.G. Applebee, *The Vesta Rowing Club 1870-1920* (n.d.); R.D. Burnell & H.R.N. Rickett, *A short history of the Leander Club 1818 to 1968* (1968), 7, 16, 19; Donelan, 147-9; WBN, 2/4/1965, p.10, 1/1/1987, p.10.
8. Dodd, 9-12.
9. Dodd, 74.
10. [E.E. Guthrie], *The old houses of Putney* (1870), 55.
11. Dodd, 75.
12. Lloyd-Taylor, 27, 29-30.
13. Lloyd-Taylor, 22-7; Dodd, 63-4.

Putney at Play

1 Gerhold, *Putney in 1636*, 16.
2. SRO, 176/2/3a & 5.
3. WLHC, Petty Sessions minutes, 1786-1830.
4. PRO, C5/85/96.
5. *The Antiquarian Magazine and Bibliographer* (1882) II, 58-9.
6. WLHC, Putney poor rates, 1741.
7. Guildhall Library, MS 11936, vol. 16, p.185; WLHC, Petty Sessions minutes.
8. WH, forthcoming.
9. WLHC, Petty Sessions minutes; Young & Co, deeds; WHNS 1962/3.
10. Young & Co., deeds.
11. Gerhold, *Putney in 1636*, 23; Donelan, 130.
12. Pepys' diary; *Read's Weekly Journal*, 30 Aug. 1718; Historical Manuscripts Commission, VII (1879), 506.
13. J. Goulstone, *Early club and village cricket* (1972).
14. CRW 1, 412.
15. NRO, SOX 169, correspondence 1774-1887, Mr Drummond 1857.
16. WBN, 21/3/1887.
17. Roehampton Cricket Club, *Towards the second century* (1951); *Putney Cricket Club: a short history, 1870-1959* (1959); WBN, 26/4/1963, p.2; WH 6 (1972) 5-6; Goulstone.
18. J. Ryan, *The annals of the Thames Hare and Hounds 1868 to 1945* (1968), 1; *The Times*, 13/1/1960.
19. Putney Lawn Tennis Club, *Centenary special 1879-1979* (1979).
20. WLHC, Putney Elected Vestry minutes, 10 July & 11 Sept 1884.
21. Donelan, 152.
22. *Historical Manuscripts Commission*, V (1876), 168.
23. Donelan, 167.
24. WBN, 1/8/1958, p.11; WHNS 1959/5.
25. Donelan, 34.
26. Brown, *Richmond Park*, 150-5.
27. Rosslyn Park R.F.C., commemorative booklet (1957).
28. WH 47 (1986), 7-10; WBN, 11/8/1894, p.4, 19/4/1963, p.14.
29. WBN, 3/9/1965, p.9, 19/11/1965, p.15.
30. WBN, 18/5/1973, p.13.
321 WBN, 17/2/1961, p.7.
32. WBN, 24/2/1911, p.5; WLHC, list of cinemas.

Putney at Prayer

1. CWA 1, f.4.
2. Edward Sclater, *Account of his public recantation* (1689).
3. LPL, VP II/2/1.
4. WH 45 (1985), 15; Basil F.L. Clarke, *Parish*

churches of London (1966), 257.
5. LPL, MS 1134-6, vol. 2; LPL, VP II/2/1.
6. LPL, VP I/1/8/1; LPL, VP II/2/2b.
7. PRO, RG4/2889; Edward E. Cleal, *The story of Congregationalism in Surrey* (1908), 234-9.
8. P.C.B. Wallis, *Saint Margaret's, Putney Park Lane* (1959), 6.
9. B. Clarke, 258.
10. WH 10 (1974), 1-11.
11. Wallis.
12. Leslie Farmer, *The Putney story: a history of Putney Methodism* (1970); Yseult Bridges, *Poison and Adelaide Bartlett* (1962); Booth, vol. 5, 211-12.
13. WH 9 (1973), 9; *Kelly's Directory*, 1914/15.
14. WH 9 (1973), 9; Booth, 210.
15. Ordnance Survey 50" map, c1903.
16. Booth, 210-15.
17. Richard Mudie-Smith, *The religious life of London* (1904).
18. WH 56 (1988), 1-4.
19. B. Clarke, 257.
20. Mother Hilary Davidson, 'History of Elm Grove, Roehampton', Part 2, *The Chronicle of Digby Stuart College* (1959), 21, 23.
21. Davidson, part 4 (1961); Alcock, 77-114; WLHC, local enquiries, St Mary's Convent.
22. *Kelly's Directory*, 1889, 1914/15; Alcock, 106; Booth, 98.
23. See local directories; WLHC, card index.

Educating Putney

1. PRO, PROB 11/378, q.162.
2. Joan Frawley, *The Watermen's School, 1684-1911* (unpub. thesis, 1975), 32, 27-28 (copy in Wandsworth Museum).
3. SRO, Quarter Sessions rolls, Easter 1679.
4. CWA 2, ff. 156, 163, 177.
5. Frawley, 34; LPL, VH 96/2079.
6. LPL, VP II/2/1; Daniel Lysons, *Supplement to the first edition of the historical account of the environs of London* (1811), 61-2.
7. Lysons, *Supplement*, 61-2.
8. Parliamentary Papers, 1819 IX part 2.
9. LPL, VP II/2/2b.
10. *A Charge on the Parish*, WP 1, 63; Lysons, *Supplement*, 61-2.
11. *Treasurer's report of the Putney & Roehampton National Schools* (1830); C. Ouvry, *A study of the church schools in the parish of Putney 1836 to 1936* (unpub. thesis), 34.
12. Ouvry, 22-4, 47; Parliamentary Papers, 1835 XLIII.
13. WH 18 (1978), 4; Parliamentary Papers, 1835 XLIII; CRW 1.
14. WH 8 (1973), 7-8.
15. PRO, ED 3/16.
16. Ralph M. Wardle, *Mary Wollstonecraft* (1951), 103-4, 107, 122.
17. *Putney 1851*, 20; LPL, VP 1C/1c/20.
18. *Putney 1851*,10; Bodleian Library, G.A. Surrey 8° 176; E. Hammond, *Bygone Putney* (1898) 57.
19. Ouvry, 26; WBN, 12/11/1954, pp. 8, 17.
20. Ouvry, 39.

Modern Putney

1. LCC, *London housing* (1937), 139-43.
2. LCC, *Names of streets and places in the administrative County of London* (4th edn., 1955).
3. Gordon D. Ramsay, *Changing Putney* (unpub. thesis, 1950, in possession of P.K. Gerhold), based on LCC Housing Dept records.
4. WLHC, insurance company map, 1907.
5. WH 55 (1988), 8-15.
6. Smiths Industries, *K.L.G. – from cars to Concorde* (1989).
7. 1981 census, Greater London abstract.
8. WBN, 29/6/1956, 11/11/1960, 1/11/1957, 4/6/1965.

INDEX

Illustrations are denoted by an asterisk